Martina Handler

Retelling the Nicaraguan Revolution as a Dionysian Ritual

Die kommende Demokratie

herausgegeben
von

Wolfgang Dietrich
(Universität Innsbruck)

Band 3

LIT

Martina Handler

Retelling the Nicaraguan Revolution as a Dionysian Ritual

About the Rise and Fall of a Partnership Society

LIT

Gedruckt mit Unterstützung des Bundesministeriums
für Wissenschaft und Forschung in Wien

Das Land
Steiermark
→ Wissenschaft und Forschung

Bibliographic information published by the Deutsche Nationalbibliothek
The Deutsche Nationalbibliothek lists this publication in the Deutsche Nationalbibliografie; detailed bibliographic data are available in the Internet at http://dnb.d-nb.de.

ISBN 978-3-643-50097-7

A catalogue record for this book is available from the British Library

Krotenthallergasse 10/8
A-1080 Wien
Tel. +43 (0) 1-409 56 61
Fax +43 (0) 1-409 56 97
e-Mail: wien@lit-verlag.at
http://www.lit-verlag.at

LIT VERLAG Dr. W. Hopf
Berlin 2010
Fresnostr. 2
D-48159 Münster
Tel. +49 (0) 2 51-620 320
Fax +49 (0) 2 51-922 60 99
e-Mail: lit@lit-verlag.de
http://www.lit-verlag.de

Distribution:
In Germany: LIT Verlag Fresnostr. 2, D-48159 Münster
Tel. +49 (0) 2 51-620 32 22, Fax +49 (0) 2 51-922 60 99, e-Mail: vertrieb@lit-verlag.de

In Austria: Medienlogistik Pichler-ÖBZ GmbH & Co KG
IZ-NÖ, Süd, Straße 1, Objekt 34, A-2355 Wiener Neudorf
Tel. +43 (0) 22 36-63 53 52 90, Fax +43 (0) 22 36-63 53 52 43, e-Mail: mlo@medien-logistik.at

In Switzerland: B + M Buch- und Medienvertriebs AG
Hochstr. 357, CH-8200 Schaffhausen
Tel. +41 (0) 52-643 54 30, Fax +41 (0) 52-643 54 35, e-Mail: order@buch-medien.ch

In the UK by: Global Book Marketing, 99B Wallis Rd, London, E9 5LN
Phone: +44 (0) 20 8533 5800 – Fax: +44 (0) 1600 775 663
http://www.centralbooks.co.uk/html

In North America by:

Transaction Publishers
New Brunswick (U.S.A.) and London (U.K.)

Transaction Publishers
Rutgers University
35 Berrue Circle
Piscataway, NJ 08854

Phone: +1 (732) 445 - 2280
Fax: + 1 (732) 445 - 3138
for orders (U. S. only):
toll free (888) 999 - 6778
e-mail: orders@transactionpub.com

The true revolutionary is guided by feelings of love.

(Ché Guevara)

Aber ich meine, dass man zu irgendeinem Zeitpunkt im Leben die Revolution von ihrem hässlichen Sockel holen sollte, um ihr die Größe des Alltäglichen zurückzugeben, des Realen, der winzigen Individuen, die wir alle mit unserem Körper, unseren Träumen und Empfindungen sind. Wir haben doch die Schnauze schon gestrichen voll von all diesen ach so moralischen Akteuren wie Vaterland, Revolution, Partei, Geschichte – alle hoch oben auf dem Sockel –, und alle haben sich in der Praxis zur Genüge als unmoralisch erwiesen. Es ist notwendig, hinzugehen und aus der Nähe zu sehen, wie die wirklichen Menschen, die sich hinter diesen aufgeplusterten Worten verbergen, leben, wovon sie träumen und wie sie sich lieben und miteinander schlafen.

(Debray in Garcia Marquez 2000: 224)

TABLE OF CONTENTS

INTRODUCTION 8
I. Transpersonal Approaches to Conflict Transformation: ....
An Introduction into Systems Thinking 13
I.1 Conflict Transformation 14
I.2 Nietzsche's Dionysus: An archetypal principle of human existence 18
I.2.1 Tracing the roots: Nietzsche and Schopenhauer 19
I.2.2 The Dionysian World View 20
I.2.3 Dionysian Ecstasy as Healing and Unity 27
I.2.4 Honoring Both Gods in Kind 29
I.2.5 Nietzsche and Freud - an Alliance against Reason 31
I.3 C.G. Jung's concept of the Collective Unconscious 35
I.4 Systems Philosophy: an Interconnected Humanity 41
I.4.1 99 and 1 Monkey 42
I.4.2 The World as an Interconnected System 47
I.4.3 The human organism as a system based on cooperation 52
I.4.3.1 "Die stärkste und beste Droge für den Menschen ist der andere Mensch" 55
I.4.3.2 The role of aggression 56
I.4.3.3 Preconditions for a successful relationship 57
I.5 Cultures of Peace(s). Partnership versus Dominance 59
I.5.1 The Time of the Great Mother 60
I.5.1.1 The Crete Phenomenon 62
I.5.1.2 System stability and system change 63
I.5.1.3 The hierarchic holdback 65
I.5.2 A History of Peace? 66
I.5.3 Partnership 69

II. NICARAGUA - A CASE STUDY ON REVOLUTION 71
Household Earth and Principle Hope 71
II.2 The Nicaraguán Revolution as a Dionysian Ritual 73
II.2.1 Myths and Archetypes 75
II.2.1.1 The Fallen Hero (A fairy tale) 78
II.2.1.2 Motherhood 81
II.2.2 Ecstasy and Chaos 86
II.2.3 Creativity 90
II.2.4 Equality 93
II.3 The "New Nicaragua" as a Transrational System 96
II.3.1 How did the System work? 96
II.3.2 Why did the System collapse? A Feminist Interpretation. 98
II.2.2.1"Quien te quiere, te aporrea."The Role of Machismo 104
II.3.2.2 Promiscuity 110
II.3.3 The Aftermath: Emerging Consciousness 115
II.3.4 A different vision 117
II.4 Idealization 119
THE DREAM ALIVE 127
BIBLIOGRAPHY 132

INTRODUCTION

The idea to write about this rather unusual topic came to my mind after I had finished my third term of the MA Program for Peace, Development, Security and International Conflict Transformation in Innsbruck in August 2006. But in reality, the topic chose me long ago, after I visited Nicaragua for the first time in 2004, when I couldn't stop reading more and reflecting more on Nicaragua and the Nicaraguans. I personally experienced this mobilizing energy which to a certain degree is still there, and after all that I learned about transrational approaches, I believe could be re-awakened. I experienced the 25th commemoration of the revolution in Managua, and being in the middle of this crowd of thousands and thousands of chanting people, I got caught by some kind of surreal reality I never experienced before. I asked myself, if it could be that the dream of a revolution was never really given up by all these people, who once were caught in this all-encompassing, utopian dome of hope?

In Nicaragua, I had the quite special chance to get to know something about the people and their way of living, working directly with a group of committed women who strive for women's empowerment through education and intellectual advancement[1].

After writing a research paper on Nicaragua applying the very useful approach of Hardt's and Negri's Empire[2], I felt that the postmodern way of perceiving the world didn't capture my personal standing towards Nicaragua well enough; and I couldn't convince myself that to unfold the obscured techniques of Empire, of the momentous external influences and power struggles, would satisfy my need to look beyond the "invisible" structures and processes that are, without any doubt, of high importance and influence the world in manifold ways, as they also shape our own perspectives and ideas.

In short, to focus "only" on the external factors and on the structures behind them couldn't capture for me what might have happened in the Nicaraguan revolution in 1979. And the meaning of the revolution itself, what is left from it in today's Nicaragua, what is left from it in people's

---

[1] I want to thank the organization MIRIAM Austria for their hospitality and for their work which they do with great commitment and enthusiasm.

[2] Michael Hardt and Antonio Negri (2000) understand empire as a hybrid, deterritorialized network of capital-strong power structures.

minds and their ways of living and seeing the world, is what interests me the most. I think it is a valuable contribution to peace research to take a closer look at the individuals who made the revolution possible, and at the systemic processes that connected them in their dreams and encouraged them to go and fight for the realization of those.

The fascination that is connected with the idea of revolution and with its realization in Nicaragua is therefore the starting point of my book. The theoretical and methodological framework I'm going to apply is characterized by a complex web of interrelated approaches, and my main objective cannot be more than to draw a more or less holistic picture of this web.

My main idea is to show how a high level of transformative energy was accumulated in the Nicaraguan society over time and partly by transpersonal means, based on a common, maybe utopian, vision of a more just, equal and prosperous future for everybody, that led to a general vision of Nicaragua as a partnership-oriented community of people standing up against a suppressive dominator-system (the dictatorial regime of the Somoza family, which was ruling the country in a dynastic manner for more than forty years). This powerful image led the revolution to immediate success through an energetic upheaval that can be analyzed as a ritual in the Dionysian sense.

The image of the revolution as a powerful ritual strongly connected with the Dionysian values of association, collective identity, the suspension of hierarchies that separate people by social status, sex, race, ethnic group etc. as well as the notion of collective *ecstasy* and its erotic components furthermore traveled across the world and fascinated people in the west who strengthened the utopianism by attributing an ideological, romantic aspect to it. The desire for a way of life where the Dionysian or energetic principle and the Apollonian or ordering principle are balanced and allowed to coexist and complement each other is understood as the expression of a reality that has been lost long ago in western societies.

The capacity to imagine a different future is crucial for any kind of society transformation. To make change happen, we need energy, creativity and collective spirit - principles that are represented by the Dionysian. The need to order and structure in the organization of society is understood as the need for the Apollonian side of human identity. These principles can be applied for individuals as well as groups, or in other words, it reconnects the individual with the collective, since there is none without the other.

As the story of Nicaragua goes on after the immediate revolutionary victory, we observe the difficulties the new leadership faced with the implementation of the Dionysian principle in the daily life structures; every form of organization needs structures, with its institutions and documents, rights and duties of the citizens etc. Elise Boulding calls it the impossibility to bring the *need for order* and the *desire for connectedness with nature* together, a problem that utopian transformation movements frequently face in the stage of realizing/implementing their visions into a state structure (Boulding E. 2000: 36).

If it is at all possible to set up a societal order where each and every individual is recognized as an important link of the whole so that the societal system is in balance, then how can this balance be stabilized? By reading testimonials and fictitious (including utopian) writings by female and feminist authors as well as contemporary reports of western witnesses through the lens of systemic approaches, I hope to contribute in some ways to answering this question.

The book at hand is characterized by some serious limitations. First, the application of the herewith developed theoretical framework on the Nicaraguan situation has to be considered an experiment that has never been attempted before. Second, the case study cannot fulfill the criteria of really presenting the full picture due to my conscious decision to focus on the stories of women (which is excluding to a great extent the voices of men); furthermore, due to the methodology of the case study which is thoroughly qualitative and therefore cannot be seen as representative, and my attempt to let Nicaraguan women speak for themselves is in addition limited through the availability of sources, which led to a selection of protagonists that maybe could be called elitist - in other words, I couldn't capture the stories of the *campesinas*, the countrywomen, or the factory workers since I was not able to go to Nicaragua myself to do first-hand research for this book.

On the other hand, I never aimed at developing a full political or historical analysis of the occurrences in Nicaragua from the 1960ies until today. On the contrary, I would like to see this book as a valuable addition to the numerous excellent scientific, personal, artistic etc. documents, publications and testimonials that already exist on the topic of Nicaragua. I believe that my attempt to understand the Nicaraguan revolution as a Dionysian ritual, which was celebrated as a state of transition with the objective to transcend the old, hierarchic-patriarchal order and create a totally new Nicaragua based on a completely different vision of a societal system organized in a partnership-way, where the Dionysian and the Apollonian aspects of human nature were honored in kind and its members learned to relate to each other with dignity and respect, aiming to build a world where every human being and nature itself was granted the same right to live and flourish, is adding a new perspective to the existing literature on revolution and social change theories.

The structure of this book is as follows: In the first part, the theoretical-methodical framework is discussed starting with the concept of *conflict transformation* as a new paradigm in peace and conflict studies that understands conflict as a necessary prerequisite for social change and applies an energetic approach. The next subchapter is dealing with the Dionysian world view as described and used by Friedrich Nietzsche. The subtitle *An archetypal principle of human existence* already anticipates the passage to the next subchapter, *C. G. Jung's concept of the collective unconscious* which is, following a discussion of the discovery of the unconscious by Sigmund Freud and how his findings are related to Nietzsche, understanding Jung's transcendence of Freud's proposals onto a transpersonal level as a true paradigm shift in experimental science. His archetype theory as directly connected to the idea of a collective unconscious of humanity sheds a new light on Nietzsche's Dionysus and Apollo. The discussion now turns to *Systems Philosophy* and the understanding of humanity as interconnected through time and space. Scientists like Rupert Sheldrake who try to prove Jung's theories through scientific experiments contribute to this field of study as much as philosophers like Ervin Laszlo and Kenneth Boulding, who go further in analyzing the world as a system constituted by uncountable subsystems. Finally, Joachim Bauer's innovative approach of using recent neurobiological findings that point out that the human organism is a system made for cooperation rather than competition will be taken further in the next subchapter, *Cultures of Peace(s). Partnership versus Dominance*, with the approaches of Riane Eisler and David Loye who with very different means disprove and reinterpret Darwinism which they see as being (mis)used to teach humanity that our evolution is based on an individual *struggle for survival*, where we are all competing against each other. Eisler's Cultural Transformation Theory uses archaeological material, which gives evidence that in prehistoric times, human societies were organized as partnership-oriented, relational and energetic communities, which stands in sharp contrast to our current world order based on dominance and hierarchy. Elise Boulding emphasizes the need for dreams and utopian visions and adds stories of successful social change from a dominator to a partnership society.

The second part of the book deals with the Nicaraguan revolution as such, by first examining the revolutionary struggle and victory as a Dionysian ritual including myths and archetypes used as community-creating principles. By analyzing two such archetypes, the hero (or fallen hero as in the case of Edén Pastora) and the motherhood archetype, it can already be seen how these myths that created images of collectivism and strength were also counterproductive regarding the construction of an ideal society, where gender stereotypes have no place. Other key aspects of a Dionysian ritual: *Ecstasy and chaos, creativity and equality* are discussed using exemplary quotations of women who experienced this time as active participants. Secondly, the questions *How did the System work*? and *Why did the System collapse?* are discussed and the book offers a feminist interpretation of the collapse, showing how the Dionysian and female elements were pushed out more or less immediately and how the system of machismo prevented a deeper transformation of the social system which would have to start (and not, as it happened, stop in front of) the homes and the family relations. Subsequently, it can be shown how the collapse of the system can also be understood as a necessary step towards the full liberation of women and the development of a feminist consciousness which finally may lead to the emergence of a totally new, partnership-oriented vision of power and society. The third subchapter of the second part uses a testimonial of an Austrian man, Dietmar Schönherr, traveling to Nicaragua to show how the revolution and its ideals have been received in a romanticized and idealized way in the western world which is understood as a symptom of the void in the minds and hearts of people, after the Dionysian elements have been demonized in the western culture.

I. Transpersonal Approaches to Conflict Transformation: An Introduction into Systems Thinking

Transpersonal and transrational approaches to conflict transformation are based on an energetic understanding of peace: An understanding of peace, connected with the ancient cosmovision of the Earth as the Great Mother, or *Gaia*, as the Earth Goddess was called in ancient Greece, who is naturally connected with harmony, fertility, and femininity. The Gaia hypothesis[3], a scientific approach also referred to as *earth systems theory*, furthermore allows us to see the world as a "great body of interacting systems" (Boulding E. 2000: 189). This new stream of thought in natural sciences helps us in my point of view to re-connect the theories of transpersonal psychology, a school of thought that works on the so-called transrational, complex web of interconnections of all human beings beyond time and space limits, with a holistic, "scientific" (according to the ruling principle of rational, facts-based science) systems theory. The fact that the term used for this new scientific perspective on life and the world as a whole, Gaia, is also a metaphor for the ancient world view that understood the world as a living organism, the "Great Mother", connected to fertility, femininity and harmony, as stated above, and human beings as one part of a bigger reality, of a greater system, could indeed make way for a paradigm shift towards a more energetic world view; a world view that would embrace complexity and be aware of the interconnectedness of not only humanity, but the whole. A world view that would re-animate an old wisdom that, according to Riane Eisler (1988), once existed among various human societies in prehistoric times: "This is that in all these places where the first great breakthroughs in our material and social technology were made [...] God was a woman" (Eisler 1988: 12). According to Eisler, most archaeologists just ignored the evidence or made a pass-by remark about the astonishing discovery that these ancient societies were organized in an egalitarian, partnership-oriented way, much different from what we've been told over and over again by scientists. Eisler highlights that Marija Gimbuta, author of *"The Goddesses and Gods of Old Europe"*, a pioneer

[3] "The gaia hypothesis, that the Earth's living matter, air, oceans, and land surface form a complex system that can be seen as a single organism having the capacity to keep our planet a fit place for life, was first developed by James E. Lovelock in *Gaia, A New Look at Life on Earth (New York: Oxford Univ. Press, 1979)."* (Boulding E. 2000: 294)

archaeologist, was the first one to bring this fact to public attention, "that in these societies we see no signs of the sexual inequality we have been taught is only 'human nature'" (Eisler 1988: 14).

According to Wolfgang Dietrich (2006a), this energetic cosmovision was part of most ancient cultures, including European cultures. But with the emergence of the concept of negative peace as the absence of war, the Mediterranean cultures developed a completely different world view which was, thanks to Plato, based on the inflexible and "stubborn" assumption of the *One Truth*. This conviction started to rule over the relational concepts of harmony and communication, and Europe lost its energetic aspects based on relation and communication. Dietrich argues, that this development, which was directly leading to the birth of modern science and the scientific world view was, on the one hand, the beginning of Europe's economic superiority but, on the other hand, it was also the beginning of the inability of Europeans to transform conflicts in a relational way, by means of communication and negotiation. Rationality started not only to rule over creativity, but it came to be the only accepted way of perceiving the world. The loss of all the other ways of perceiving the world left a hole in what has once been a holistic way of living.

I.1 Conflict Transformation

The term "conflict transformation" has been widely accepted as an alternative concept in peace studies for the last couple of years or even decades, and in my point of view, it is quite telling that initiatives like the well-known German *Berghof Research Center for Constructive Conflict Management* recently (in 2004) founded a new foundation, called the *Berghof-Foundation for Peace Support,* which proposes "systemic conflict transformation" (2006) instead of conflict resolution or conflict management. All this seems to confirm a paradigm shift in the discipline of peace and conflict studies, based on the principal understanding that conflicts are, always have been, and always will be a crucial part of human existence, and that to resolve or abolish them therefore cannot be a realistic goal, and should not be a desired objective.

John Paul Lederach states that "conflict is normal in human relationships and conflict is a motor of change" (Lederach 2003: 4). Conflict is therefore relational; hence if there were no human relationships, conflict would not exist. Lederach understands the term "transformation" as a process towards healthier relationships and communities, which demands active changes in our ways of relating to each other. In the first chapter of his recent book, *The moral imagination. The art and soul of building peace (2005),* Lederach formulates a question that leads his research and work, as he says, and it also captures the core message of conflict transformation for me: "How do we transcend the cycles of violence that bewitch our human community while still living in them?" (Lederach 2005: 4-5). For Lederach, this is only possible when we understand conflict as something positive and constructive, as it helps us to first identify the deeply rooted injustices in a society, and then to advocate deep societal changes towards justice, respect for human rights and life, and towards healthier relationships and social structures based on these values and on the principle of nonviolence.

Although there are many different approaches that use the term "conflict transformation", they all have one thing in common: The belief in the possibility for social change that involves more than the immediate or visible actors and conflict parties, and more than the immediately visible conflict situation. "This contrasts with problem-solving conflict resolution, which is used to resolve a specific short-term problem, while usually ignoring or avoiding long-term relationship issues" (Burgess & Burgess 1997). Lederach uses a simple example to explain that difference: a discussion or fight in a family about whose turn it is to wash the dishes. Conflict resolution, he says, would mean to find an immediate solution for the superficial problem: somebody has to wash the dishes, and there are many ways of assigning this task to somebody by giving different arguments. Most of the time, Lederach tells us, this is what happens in his own family - due to the lack of time or interest, the conflict remains and gets solved on a superficial level. But conflict transformation requires to look deeper, and to see the questions and assumptions of every involved individual that lay behind the visible dispute.

> We are negotiating the nature and quality of our relationship, our expectations of each other, our interpretations of our identity as individuals and as a family, our sense of self-worth and care for each other, and the nature of power and decision-making in our relationship. (Lederach 2003: 11)

This example already leads to a systemic perspective, which could also be described as a way of "looking as well as seeing" (Lederach 2003: 9); a perspective that strives to see more than we can grasp with our eyes; a view that links the collective and the individual well-being together and emanates from an energetic understanding of human relations and, consequently, of peace. Systemic conflict transformation recognizes that there is a pattern in the ups and downs, the energetic flows of human relationships, which can, if we acknowledge it, help us to understand a certain up or down, peak or valley, as Lederach calls it, of individual or collective relations e.g. of conflicts. To apply a systemic perspective means to look for the full picture instead of hastily jumping to conclusions.

Conflict transformation also involves complexity, another important term when we talk about energetic approaches to peace and conflict. Simplified "either/or" choices are not really applicable in complex and contradictory circumstances that define human relations, especially in times of extremely high energy density, like on the peak of a conflict. "Complexity requires that we develop the capacity to identify the key energies in a situation and hold them up together as **interdependent goals**" (Lederach 2003: 52). To appreciate complexity helps us resist the idea that we can "solve" a conflict or problem so that in the end, it becomes an orderly package, which is also logically consistent. This is not how human relationships work, let alone in a state of high energies status.

Coming back to the idea of conflict transformation as an alternative program to conflict resolution and management, the energetic approach is crucial to guarantee the flexibility and creativity of this new way of dealing with conflicts. Exactly because the energetic perspective is incorporated in all conflict transformation approaches, there are so many different ones, or, to put it the other way round, there can never be one right way of conflict transformation, as there is no one nature of conflicts nor one definite state of peace.

> The decisive factor is to no longer perceive conflict as an immoral opposite to negative peace but rather as a positive sign of social energy. This energy can then be extracted through non-violent means in order to transform problematic situations. Under this proposition, key terms of international politics such as conflict prevention, peace building, peace keeping or even peace enforcement no longer make sense but are shown to block the potentially positive energy of conflict. (Dietrich 2006a: 33)

Also the Norwegian "Father of Peace Studies" Johan Galtung uses the term "conflict transformation". His *transcend* approach is a highly energetical approach. The main idea is that conflicts can be "transcended" by creativity - by envisioning a new order of things, for example society. "By 'transcendence' we mean creating a new type of reality. Something that potentially was always there is becoming empirical reality" (Galtung 2000: 30). Like Lederach, Galtung advocates complexity and to understand a conflict by taking into account ALL its layers and players. The transcend framework understands conflict not only as normal in human relationships, but also as something that can have positive and negative, creative and destructive effects. This idea derives from an energetic world view: conflict is a status of high energy, and energy is always neutral, and can be used for better or worse. Galtung also refers to "conflict energy" as high energy with a great transformative potential. Couldn't this potential be used for more constructive, meaningful aims? "Those who enter conflict should have ambitious meta-goals, like a better Yugoslavia, peace and development in the Middle East, reduction of misery in Peru, etc" (Galtung 2000: 31). Social revolutions are meant to carry out highly ambitious, ideological changes. The meta-goals in the Nicaraguan revolution for example were quite clear - it was easy to understand from the inside and even from the outside, what the *Sandinista National Liberation Front*[4] was fighting against.

There is one part in Galtung's *transcend* approach which I consider most important for this book: the strong emphasis on *creativity* that he makes over and over again. Without creativity, conflict transformation seems not possible. Because change needs creativity, and creativity needs energy and the capacity to look beyond and see the full picture. We could say that creativity is the energetic drive behind every transformation, or transcendence, as Galtung likes to call it. He talks about "lifting up" the conflict onto another level: a less violent, more creative or we could also say: more complex level of human coexistence. This last remark leads us directly towards a system-theoretical approach of human relations.

---

[4] The Sandinista National Liberation Front, FSLN (Frente Sandinista de Liberación Nacional) was founded in 1961 in Nicaragua. The name refers to Augusto César Sandino, a revolutionary, who led the first anti-imperialist liberation struggle in Nicaragua in the 1930ies. After the victory of the revolution, the FSLN constituted the ruling party.

I.2 Nietzsche's Dionysus: An archetypal principle of human existence

The German philosopher Friedrich Nietzsche (1844-1900) strikingly supports the view of a momentous "loss" in European history (e.g. Eisler 1988, Dietrich 2006a) in his work *"The Birth of Tragedy"* (Nietzsche 1999a). There he states that this loss came about, when the two Greek Gods, Apollo and Dionysus, the God of form and the God of energy, two fundamental principles that form the two sides of human reality, were separated. Other than his forerunners like the art historian J. J. Winckelmann or the renown writer G. E. Lessing, who saw the development of Greek tragedy as an evolutionary development from a more primitive, emotional, to a more rational, logical world view, Nietzsche argues that the unique "pairing" of these two opposites, these two parts of an ever-reproducing duality, took place in ancient Greece with the development of *Attic tragedy.* He calls this event when the two opposite Gods complemented each other a "metaphysical miracle of the Hellenic 'Will'" (Nietzsche 1999a: 14).

> Instead of regarding the dark and sinister side of Greek art as an underdeveloped or aberrant aspect of the Greek world-view that leads to a higher, truer, more rational and optimistic attitude, Nietzsche insists that this rational and optimistic character was actually nothing more than a relatively late and thoroughly artificial representation of a more basic, instinctive, and fundamentally aesthetic view of human existence. It is only when both of these seemingly mutually exclusive attitudes are brought together that we can achieve a complete and "whole" picture of the ancient Greek world-view. (Sweet 1999: 352)

Nietzsche concludes that Greek tragedy developed directly out of the Athenian festival called Dionysia, held in honor of the god Dionysus, the god of organic nature, ecstasy, instinct, and fertility. According to Nietzsche, the purpose of this festival was to bring the inhabitants of Athens into an altered state of consciousness, "whereby the ordinary sense of individuality is lost and an aesthetic experience of the wholeness and unity of nature is achieved" (Sweet 1999: 354). With the structuring of the staged tragedy, the Apollonian ordering principle was added to the wild orgies in honor of Dionysus.

I.2.1 Tracing the roots: Nietzsche and Schopenhauer

According to Sokel, Nietzsche owed the very foundation of his thought to the German philosopher Arthur Schopenhauer (1788-1860). And indeed, Nietzsche's use of the concept of the "Will" clearly derives from Schopenhauer who "saw what he called the Will as the motor and perennial substratum of all being" (Sokel 2006:1). But Nietzsche reinterpreted the extremely pessimistic philosophy of Schopenhauer, for whom the all-encompassing, all-producing Will leads to a pessimistic world view since there is nothing except the Will (The *World as Will)* and the Will can never be satisfied lastingly. The result is an infinite impulse to want, seek and desire, while "it could never give lasting happiness or even contentment to individual beings" (Sokel 2006: 2). The only way to escape the Will temporarily is in Platonic illusions (The *World as Representation*).

Nietzsche's interpretation of the Will turns it 360 degrees around and he manages to develop a radically optimistic vitality out of the pessimism Schopenhauer stands for. For Nietzsche, the Will is embodied in the Greek god Dionysus, who represents the infinite energy of life and the cosmic unity of all beings. But for Nietzsche, Dionysus is more than that, yet he is both: *Will* and *Representation* (Sokel 2006: 3).

The example he uses to develop this theory further is Greek tragedy. For Nietzsche, the main accomplishment of Greek tragedy is the unity of the two opposite principles of humanity: Apollo and Dionysus, energy and form. He explains how in Greek tragedy the individuals are shown as victims of the Will, as sufferers of life as such, that outwits them and leads them into hopeless, unbearable situations. But where Schopenhauer saw it as the root of his ultimate pessimism, that individuals are nothing outside the Will and while they seem to take individual decisions, they have to realize, that in the end the Will doesn't give them a choice and they find themselves in the famous dead end situations of an unsolvable interpersonal conflict (personal relations against prevalent moral rules/taboos), Nietzsche interprets Greek tragedy differently, since for him, the individual tragic personalities are not the only focus points of tragedy, but there is also always the chorus, without which the art form would not be imaginable.

> (T)ragedy as a form, a performance, transcends the tragic spectacle it shows. It transcends it in the chorus. For the chorus, representation of the collective life, the universal, the cosmic unity

> of being, survives the fall of individual heroes. The chorus has the last word and with it proclaims the consoling message of Dionysianism: 'Life goes on. Individuals come and go, rise and fall, but being as a whole is everlasting. The individual dies, and that is tragic. But being goes on for ever and ever', and therein lies the profound metaphysical consolation of tragedy. (Sokel 2006: 4)

I.2.2 The Dionysian World View

In his essay on the Dionysian world view, Nietzsche goes further into detail in explaining how in his opinion Greek tragedy by including the Dionysian aspect of human reality into a society based on the Apollonian world of the Olympic Gods, a world of *beautiful semblance* ("schöner Schein") and optimism, had overcome duality in a way.

To make this a bit more understandable, I will try to roughly outline the differences between Apollonian and Dionysian art and world view, as elaborated by Nietzsche. Apollo, the god of form, is the god of *dream-representations.* This choice of words that Nietzsche uses is very self-explanatory as it shows us what the Apollonian is not very familiar with: truth and reality. The Apollonian strives for perfection (perfect *forms*). The art forms that are to be considered Apollonian are the art of the sculptor, or image-creator, and the Homeric epic. Image-creators, sculptors, as well as epic poets are seeking perfect forms of a kind that never exist in nature and in real life. The artists can be seen as God-like individuals, who are elevated over the rest of the people. The Apollonian world view is therefore based on an enormous illusion, Nietzsche states: the Olympian gods represent the Apollonian attributes: beauty, tranquility and pleasure. He goes on that the Olympian world and with it their gods were created out of the necessity to seduce people so that they would want to live on. As long as the Olympian world of beautiful semblance exists, there is optimism and hope that is worth living. "Under the influence of such a religion, life is understood in the Homeric world as that which is inherently desirable: life beneath the sunshine of such gods" (Nietzsche 1999b: 125).

Nietzsche calls the continuous struggle in history between the Dionysian and the Apollonian world view therefore the "struggle between truth and beauty" (Nietzsche 1999b: 126).

The Dionysian world view, on the other hand, unites human beings rather than creating a hierarchical structure (like the Apollonian does by its attempt to perfection and beauty), and so, a Dionysian ritual erases the established order of things. A Dionysian world view is therefore based on *interconnectedness* (between all human beings and also between humans and nature) and *creativity*, it "brings a new world into being at each creative moment" (Nietzsche 1999b: 122). The means to achieve this new world is ecstasy *(Rausch).* Its results, formulated by Nietzsche in the 19th century, sound like a visionary harangue by an idealist revolutionary movement of the 20th century, promoting their theories for social change:

> Not only do the festivals of Dionysos forge a bond between human beings, they also reconcile human beings and nature. [...] All the cast-like divisions, which necessity and arbitrary power have established between men, disappear; the slave is a free man, the aristocrat and the man of lowly birth unite in the same Bacchic choruses. [...] As they sing and dance, human beings express their membership of a higher, more ideal community; [...] they feel themselves to have been transformed by magic, and they really have become something different. [...] He feels himself to be a god. (Nietzsche 1999b: 120f)

The Dionysian expresses itself, like the Apollonian, through artistic means, but Dionysian arts are completely different from Apollonian arts, from means to exertion as well as their effects on people and society as a whole: the arts of Dionysus are music and lyric poetry. Instead of having the creation of a (most perfect) image as a goal (like Apollonian arts do), transforms Dionysian art the artist (who can be everybody) into a piece of art, in relation to nature. Every human being is, in this sense, a piece of art, and on the other hand, every human being can create art because creativity is an inherent quality of humanity.

This feeling of togetherness, of interconnectedness gives humans an immense power to change their own realities by realizing *who they are* and through what Nietzsche calls the *ecstasy of suffering* (Rausch des Leidens). Here, the energetic world view is ruling, with its principle that energy is always neutral and can always be used for good or bad, when Nietzsche states:

> By virtue of the omnipotence of its character, the former [ecstasy of suffering] penetrates to the innermost thoughts of nature, it recognizes the fearful drive to exist and at the same time the perpetual death of everything that comes into existence; the gods which this intoxication creates are good and evil, they resemble chance, they startle us by the sudden emergence of a plan in their

> actions, they are pitiless and without delight in beauty. They are related to truth and approximate to concepts; rarely and only with difficulty do they become concentrated in figures. (Nietzsche 1999b: 126)

Because these gods show us humans without mercy the miserable reality of our lives, mortality, and subordinate place in the universe, because they show us our own reflection, all human beings can become the same in the shadow of the pitiless truth that's shown to them in the mirror of a Dionysian ritual. "In the consciousness that follows his awakening from intoxication, he sees the terrible and absurd aspects of human existence wherever he looks; it disgusts him" (Nietzsche 1999b: 130). This is why, explains Nietzsche, the Apollonian is needed, the world of beautiful semblance, that provides a place to flee from this harsh reality and allows us to get distracted by the strive for perfection and the creation of images that cover the truth that has been uncovered during the Dionysian ritual. "The innermost purpose of a culture directed towards semblance and measure can only be the veiling of truth" (Nietzsche 1999b: 128).

In this *veiling of truth* lies the birth of modern science, which later on perfected the Apollonian art of making people believe that there is something called perfection in (human) nature, and that its rules could be discovered with the scientific method of measure. The idea that the reality of nature is something to be discovered by humans finally made humans believe that they could be god-like, for they could unveil the secrets of the universe and thus take away its terrifying uncertainty. The uncertainty of humankind though is the prospect of mortality; but with the comfortable vision of a science that could know and measure everything and discover the perfect image in the end, this ever-remaining, terrifying prospect could be covered and people would be driven by hope. The origin of science comes from this self-deception, which is the promise of perfection:

> The image-worship of Apolline *culture,* whether expressed in temples, in statues, or in the Homeric epic, had its sublime goal in the ethical demand for *measure,* which runs parallel to the aesthetic demand for beauty. It is only possible to demand measure where measure and limits are held to be *knowable.* (Nietzsche 1999b: 128)

Nietzsche's personal conviction is that the scientific approach is leading "to a restricted and unnatural view of reality. For Nietzsche, reason is not intrinsically opposed to instinct. It is merely "one fairly recent manifestation of human instinct" (Sweet 1999: 353). Here, we can see that for Nietzsche, dualism and the resort to the *one* truth, to a simplifying either-or, didn't exist, but there was only one underlying principle of human nature: life, as represented in the Dionysian world view. The Apollonian is only one of uncountable possible manifestations of this world-view. The problem came about though, when this reality was turned on its head.

Dietrich argues, that with the development of institutions, namely the Catholic Church and the states, the Dionysian world view was finally defeated and the two principles of human reality, form and energy, became Good and Evil. "Apollo and Dionysus at the beginning are like form and energy, but later they are like Christ and Satan, like good and evil" (Dietrich 2006a: 37). Robin Robertson detected this paradigm shift in the Renaissance, when the focus of philosophy started to become the outside rather than the inside of humanity, and nature became the matter of observation and description:

> During the 14th, 15th, and 16th centuries, Renaissance thinkers suddenly awoke, looked at the world with new eyes, and asked a different question: What is the nature of the world? That question caused them to turn their eyes outward toward the world and to begin to describe what they saw there. When that description led to new questions, they proposed solutions, then turned once more to the world to check the validity of their conclusions. (Robertson 1995: 2)

Robertson emphasizes that the new scientific world view that emerged was still strongly connected to religion. God was seen as the one who created the world in perfection and now left it for humans to discover God's eternal (= natural) laws. With the resulting development of Apollonian arts in the Renaissance, the Apollonian ideal of Man as a God-like creature began to re-emerge. This is how the existence of artists like Michelangelo and Da Vinci (who up to today receive worship that clearly makes them God-like) can be explained. "Medieval art dealt with humanity only in generalities; its real subject was God. Michelangelo created art that pictured not only a particular man or woman, but more than that, a heroic man or woman. Michelangelo's art cried that we could all be as the gods" (Robertson 1995: 3). Robertson describes the consecutive overtaking of the Apollonian ideals of heroic perfection and individualism and as its consequences the final repudiation of the Dionysian way of life as relational, as being consciously interconnected with the world, with our fellow human beings, and as finally being in balance within ourselves. All this, he states, got lost over the centuries and led to the sickness of the soul that psychoanalysis and later Jung's analytic psychology and transpersonal psychology attempted to cure.

But for Nietzsche, this institutionalized misinterpretation of reality started much earlier, more precisely, when Socratic rationalism was introduced into Greek tragedy. Plato explicitly criticized the way the Olympian gods were portrayed in traditional mythology and the first big tragedies written by Aeschylus in the 6th century B.C. "He was a man of deep religious sensibility, but believed the gods were fundamentally good, and thus that much of Homer and traditional mythology ought to be abandoned. Tragedy would also have to be censored" (Wiles 2000: 17). The paradigm shift happened, according to Nietzsche, starting from the plays of Euripides (5th century B.C.), which he sees as some kind of "light" or, following Wiles, "censored" version of tragedy.

> In the plays of Sophocles and Euripides, the representing becomes the represented, the mask becomes the face, the medium becomes the message. The harmony, rationality, and optimism, which characterize the Apollonian aspect of tragedy became ends in themselves and ceased to be the representations of a more basic, instinctive, and pessimistic (Dionysian) view of life. (Sweet 1999: 359)

Plato goes even further and notoriously denounces tragedy or comedy as not belonging to an ideal society (Wiles 2000: 18). This fatal epistemological shift opened the door for the further development of Europe: the creation of powerful institutions and hierarchies and a highly moral understanding of peace which didn't leave any space for different understandings of different cultures of different peaces or ways of living.

Following Dietrich (Dietrich 2006b), I would like to furthermore argue that this loss in European collective identity led to psychological mechanisms like projections of the own (emotional, spiritual, etc.), shortages into faraway utopian events like a revolution. These ethno-psychoanalytical phenomena will have to be taken into account not only for the reading of western publications on the Nicaraguan revolution and its aftermath, but I want to also explicitly underline the challenge for myself as a researcher, to not underestimate my own subjectivity, my own deeply rooted presumptions and idea(l)s, that have a lot to do with my choice to study and write about this topic.

Finally, I want to make the point, that to state that the Dionysian aspect of human reality has been suppressed and demonized in the course of European history, means at the same time to say that as a fundamental aspect of human reality, it always existed and does still exist. As we will see in the next chapter on the *collective unconscious* according to C.G. Jung and in the following chapters on transpersonal psychology, there is evidence that repressed memories of humanity are "stored" and can be accessed by all human beings.

At this point, I want to make a reference to the case-study of this book, the Nicaraguan revolution. Since Nietzsche is claiming that the legacy of the Dionysian world view is part of the human system, and following Sigmund Freud, who stated that repressed emotions survive in the subconscious and sooner or later but always return as a symptom, we could interpret social transformation movements like the Latin American revolutions as Dionysian rituals that express the desire for interconnectedness, for energetic and harmonious human relations. Nietzsche's description of a Dionysian ritual has indeed a lot to do with the image of revolution. He describes how literally everybody got involved in an overwhelming, excessive, ecstatic feeling.

> Rhythm, which had previously moved only in the simplest zig-zag pattern, now loosened its limbs for a Bacchanalian dance; *musical sound* rang out, no longer in ghost-like attenuation, but in the thousand-fold intensification of the mass and in the accompaniment of deep-voiced wind instruments. And the most mysterious thing of all occurred: here, harmony was born, which, in its movement, makes the will of nature immediately intelligible. (Nietzsche 1999b: 129)

Within this quote, two very important aspects of the revolution in Nicaragua are included: the first one is the power of the masses, the overwhelming feeling that arises when masses of people act together in the spirit of some higher goal; a feeling that most people have already experienced personally when they were participating in a big street demonstration. Reflecting on what happens there, who is not amazed about the power and energy that is involved in a big group of complete strangers standing up for the same cause? Doesn't it make us feel or in a strange way even seem to know, that everybody here feels the same about a specific issue and doesn't this common knowledge of each other increase the effectiveness of the upheaval as it adds to the transformative energy released through this kind of movement? If a crowd of unarmed and powerless citizens marching through the streets for a cause didn't mean more than what I just wrote, why would authoritarian regimes all over the world then be so frightened of such actions that they deny their people the right to stand up publicly and in groups? Transpersonal psychology as I understand it has an answer to this question as it explains that the rise of energy in such situations facilitates all those people to connect with each other and become aware of their own power as a collective. This is when harmony in the Nietzschean sense comes in: the harmony that happens when many different voices express the same desire in different ways, pace, languages etc. And this is exactly what makes demonstrations so dangerous for regimes based on authority and formalism that they have to prohibit them.

Coming back to the issue of the Nicaraguan revolution, it is needless to say that a revolution of such transformative character involves a much higher energy potential, or in other words: ecstasy and excess, than any street demonstration.

The second aspect I would like to highlight here is the aspect of Dionysian arts. Nietzsche writes about Bacchanalian dances, and musical sound that involved everybody; and about the sound of the masses that create harmony, unity in diversity. In Nicaragua, but I think apart from that, in every revolutionary movement aiming for social transformation, revolutionary music, poetry, and dance played an outstanding role. In Nicaragua, almost every second citizen claims to be a poet or novelist, so the story goes. This doesn't mean that every second Nicaraguan is a famous, internationally recognized poet. I think that it is much more a phenomenon that can be traced back to the Dionysian ideal of the art-loving, aesthetic individual who is in harmony with nature and praises nature's magnificence. As a part of nature, everybody can be an artist. This philosophy behind the revolution made it so persuading and all-encompassing. And it lead to the unique phenomenon of a country, where poets can become politicians and politicians can be poets, as was the case during the years of Sandinista leadership. "Nicaragua is described as a nation of Dreamers, Poets and Politicians..." (hospitalityclub 2007); that's how tourist agencies advertise Nicaragua. Who doesn't want to visit such a utopian place? This short line in a tourist advertisement proves that utopia consists of both - the Apollonian and the Dionysian aspects of humanity. But as Elise Boulding (2000) and others proclaim, it is exactly this nexus between the two principles, or rather the inability of many utopian movements to give enough space to both, that is responsible for the so-called "failure" of so many of these experiments in the long-term.

I.2.3 Dionysian Ecstasy as Healing and Unity

When we talk about the elimination of Dionysian elements in Western history, it's important to look behind the first criticism that emerges out of the conviction that human nature and society need both sides of human existence, the Dionysian and the Apollonian elements, in order to live wholly fulfilled lives. As I already illustrated, energy as the expression of the Dionysian in a systemic but also in a conflict transformation perspective is seen as something neutral and necessary: necessary for change, neutral because it can trigger and move forward any kind of change, whether positive or negative, "for better or worse", so to say. I also tried to emphasize the pushing out of Dionysian elements in western cultures by associating Dionysus with the evil, or in a more religious interpretation, with the devil/Satan.

But a rather dubious reputation seems to have accompanied Dionysus through all times. Although the *Dionysia* was one of the most important festivals in classical Greece, and surely enjoyed great popularity and is praised until today as the origin of the famous Greek theater performances (tragedy and comedy), the God of wine was also associated with madness and an evil force already as early as in the 8th century B.C.:

> In classical Greek society, the festivities of Dionysus - the Dionysia or Bacchaea - signified a break from the routine of every day life: a rest for the wife from her weaving and for the husband from social conformity. Nonetheless, as early as the 8th century B.C.E., the God of Wine was thought to be an ambivalent source of good and evil. In Homer, he was considered to have been "the pleasure of mortals" (Iliad, xiv. 325), but in Hesiod, his is a "bittersweet gift to men" (Shield of Hercules 400). Thus, from the very beginning of Greek poetry, Dionysus was considered both a good as well as an evil for those who abstain from his gifts. (Luz 1998)

One possible interpretation for this ambivalent stand of the Athenians towards Dionysus is his strong connection with the female principle, which is proven by his mythological female followers, the *maenads.* These women are described as mad, wild, intoxicated creatures, who "wandered the mountains in a state approaching trance" (Wiles 2000: 78) rather than worshiping him in a temple, like followers of the other gods and goddesses. Wiles also calls it an "anomaly" that a cult following a male god would be led by a female majority. These women followers of Dionysus are seen by archaeologists as Greek women freeing themselves from their limited existence in a very advanced culture that had introduced democracy without considering women as citizens. Especially at the time of the introduction of democracy, women must have suffered a heavy blow. It was a complete change of lifestyle and societal roles, including gender roles. Democracy didn't make life more egalitarian for women.

> In the democratic era, men removed themselves from the household to a new set of public spaces where the important business of life was now conducted. Women at the same time were removed from the public domain, in which citizen males paraded their equality. [...] The place of Athenian women became the home - and even within the home they were excluded from rooms where men entertained male guests. [...] We cannot tell how far women resented a political system, which reduced them to non-persons, because their voices are lost. (Wiles 2000: 69)

Only in religious ceremonies, women were still allowed to participate. So the Dionysus-cult can be imagined as somewhat popular among women in an atmosphere of total disregard and suppression. So another common name for Dionysus was Eleutherios "the liberator" for setting people, individuals, free to express themselves in a state of ecstasy or trance. But women who expressed themselves freely in an ecstatic, bodily way, and without any shame were perceived as dangerous because they were obviously "out of control". Wiles adheres: "Dionysus, god of theatre, is a god who dissolves identity in general, and gender in particular" (Wiles 2000: 78).

At this point, I want to go back to Nietzsche and his interpretation of ancient Greece: He asserted the way society in ancient Greece was structured, as a society originally engaged exclusively with form and beauty, with the perfect world of the Olympian gods. But at one certain point in history, he assumes, they allowed the Dionysian to enter this world of beautiful semblance and to attach a very enriching, ritualistic culture to it that allowed all humans, even the most marginalized ones, to release all their energies (positive or negative) and to create a oneness in diversity, where they could feel emotionally connected with everybody.

These rituals though didn't take place every day, but on specific occasions that helped the people to feel free for a while; like a valve to set off steam (carnival is the once-a-year Dionysian festival of our western civilization). The Athenian city festival *Dionysia* took place every spring, lasted for five days and was essentially a drama-contest (tragedy and comedy). It was organized in the name and honor of Dionysus, and therefore strongly connected with wine, intoxication and sexuality/fertility (for instance, huge wooden phalluses were carried through the streets of Athens). "Members of the audience were participants as much as spectators at the start of the festival. They ate meat from Dionysus' bull in the evening, they wore garlands of ivy, another emblem of the god, and of course they drank wine that was Dionysus' gift" (Wiles 2000: 32). This quote already underlines the participatory character of the festival. The day-long wine consumption prepared the ground for the ritualistic meaning of the theater performances.

> The ritual environment of a tragedy was part of its meaning. The spectators were able to look at situations from multiple points of view because they had ceremonially taken leave of immediate personal concerns. A collective affirmation of unity prepared the city to contemplate unhealed rifts within itself. An affirmation of divine power prepared the city for the recognition of human limits. The sight of slaughtered bulls on the altar prepared for the contemplation of human death. (Wiles 2000: 35)

I.2.4 Honoring Both Gods in Kind

To mention the occasional character of these important individual and collective events with their cleansing and healing functions is important since Nietzsche's Dionysus seems so much brighter and more attractive than his Apollo. But with all sympathy for this community-creating, egalitarian God who makes people feel free of any responsibilities and hardships, it should be said that without the ordering and conciliating principle of Apollo, no society could survive long. A society based only on the Dionysian principle would, according to Elise Boulding, even be vulnerable for charismatic leaders to abuse their strong connectedness with their followers and lead people who, in a constant state of very high energy, are in such a strong way connected with each other that can't think for themselves any more, into disaster and bloodshed.

In her writings about the role of utopianism for social change, Boulding impressively explains this phenomenon when she makes understood how there has always been one specifically tough problem that many utopian visionaries couldn't solve, which, and so she concludes, might be one of the main reasons for the "failure" of many utopian experiments throughout history. What Boulding calls the "passion for order", would in our conceptual framework be called the Apollonian principle of order, and what she calls the "longing for nature", for a connectedness and life in harmony with nature, is very close to a Dionysian principle of living. Almost never, though, did any revolutionary movement manage to connect these two aspects of humanity and give both their place in society, states Boulding, and the exclusive focus on either the one or the other, while both, as being archetypal principles of a harmonious, balanced life, needed to be incorporated in the new society resulted in the very failure she was talking about before.

The danger for a utopian movement focused exclusively on rationality, and order is that it becomes a technocratic society that focuses much more on the structures than on the content. "Society as a perfectly functioning mechanism can become an attractive idea. Planning becomes the central function of such a society. Everything becomes doable. Authoritarianism and military organization slip in easily" (Boulding 2000: 32).

This one-sided commitment to cold, scientific rationality obviously is at odds with the other utopian ideal, which is the organic connection with nature. The Anabaptist stream that developed out of the Catholic Church in the 13th century is a good example for such a movement. "Anabaptists taught egalitarianism, both between classes and between men and women. Working for the ideals of social justice and peace in the post-feudal era, they empowered peasants and workers alike with the tools of literacy and the skills of craft and industry" (Boulding 2000: 33). But this openness that became the standard of living in the Anabaptist tradition made its members "vulnerable to a charismatic leadership that violated their own intentions" (Boulding 2000: 33), and she exemplifies this with the well-known case of the charismatic Anabaptist leader John of Leyden, who forced the whole population of Munster (Germany) to take up his new religion and enforced his will as a god-like king, transforming society according to his ideas and keeping the population in a hopeless struggle against the whole ecclesiastic and profane leadership of their times (15th century). "Sie wollten das Paradies und brachten die Hölle" (Schneider 2004. Translation: They wanted paradise and brought hell); this short quote from the foreword of Schneider's book telling the life story of John of Leyden pretty much meets the point. The Anabaptist ideals of equality, religiousness, and freedom were cartooned by the blind overestimation of John of Leyden's own capacities and so a kingdom of fear was created instead of the desired kingdom of God.

This is the Achilles' heel of that kind of utopian lifestyles, explains Boulding. She writes about enormous bloodshed that was caused by violent uprisings of peasants and workers in the late Middle Ages, following charismatic leaders in the name of the Holy Spirit who "carried themselves and their followers away in an excess of emotionalism" (Boulding 2000: 33). So the complete lack of rationality and individualism is the other extreme, which we could also call a Dionysian society that's not being balanced with its Apollonian counterpart.

Human identity and the organization of human communities consist of an incredibly rich variety of different facets and it is exactly this extreme diversity of human nature in itself that makes humans capable of uncountable possible courses of action. But whenever one of these facets becomes the dominant one and thus pushes the others away, the societal system is out of balance. What most utopian movements aim at is to bring the balance back into the system, but very often, they themselves have to focus on one aspect that was lost in the societal order they want to overcome, so they strive to bring this lost aspect back into the system and thus counterbalance. But aside from the ideology, the real transition back to a society where all aspects of human identity are allowed to exist, where individualism and collectivism are two principles that complement rather than oppose each other, is a very difficult one and this is, according to Boulding, where most such movements fail. "One key problem of utopia writing is that all utopias have implicit political goals, but few Utopians are able to devise political strategies that do not destroy these very goals" (Boulding 2000: 30).

I.2.5 Nietzsche and Freud - an Alliance against Reason

Nietzsche's main argument goes against the main stream of thought of his time, against the enlightened optimism that developed out of the Kantian notion that humans share a common rationality, and that by accessing this common human reason, they can overcome irrational behavior that leads to phenomena like war, violence, and death - phenomena that no rational being can want to cause or live through. This idealist thinking includes the conviction that human behavior towards each other can be entirely based on the common ground, which is rationality. Rationality would tell us that it is more reasonable to discuss our differences on the (peace-) table and find, thus, ways to communicate and commerce with each other, instead of waging war. In his famous essay "An answer to the question: What is Enlightenment?" (1784), Kant made clear his theory of every person's ability to rise above irrationality and immaturity. His optimism is grounded in the idea, that if every human being used his/her rational mind, the world would be free of wars, violence, and pain inflicted by other human beings. What Kant brings down to the point: "The motto of enlightenment is therefore: Sapere aude! Have courage to use your own reason!" (Kant 1784), has shortly after become the mainstream philosophical credo for 200 years of idealist thinking up to today. With his categorical imperative, he suggests that we only need to think before acting, and think in a way that makes us recognize our connectedness and interdependence with all human beings. If we live up to that ideal, prosperity and progress would be guaranteed for everybody.

This is exactly the stream of thought Nietzsche is challenging, for he doesn't believe in rationality but argues that human actions are driven by instincts, unconscious forces. The Enlightenment project for him is weakening humanity since it's suppressing a powerful part of human reality - the world of instincts and creativity, the uninhibited action.

> Against the tendencies of bourgeois society, Nietzsche stressed that man ought to recognize the dark and mysterious world of instinct - the true life force. "Du sollst werden, der du bist," Nietzsche wrote. "You must become who you are." Excessive rationality, an over-reliance on Human Reason, does little more than smother the spontaneity necessary for creativity. For man to realize his potential, he must sever his dependence on reason and the intellect and instead, develop his instincts, drive, and will. (Kreis 2000)

Since for Nietzsche, following his own Dionysian principle that there is no moral supreme power, that there is no superior purpose of life, there can also not be valid rules of behavior or moral codes. His conclusion is that humans should recognize their condition, they must realize that there is no purpose in life, and then live according to their new consciousness free from all semblance and appearances, of which the belief in scientific knowledge is the biggest of all deceptions.

Robertson analyses how the science of mathematics, that has always been a system of relations, came to be understood as an absolute reality, and how numbers, which are defined through their relations with each other, came to be seen as real existing things. This new theory of nature was coined by Isaac Newton (1643-1728). The laws he found in nature would dominate the scientific view of the world for the coming centuries. "Newton's world was a world of absolutes: absolute space and time, and perfect, invisible particles moving in that absolute space and time" (Robertson 1995: 20).

Nietzsche's glorification of the Dionysian, or, as we could also call it, the transrational principle, had a strong impact on the theories of Sigmund Freud (1856-1939), who had also discovered the "dark" side of the human mind in his clinical experiences. Although Freud never publicly admitted throughout his life that he had been influenced by Nietzsche and even denied having read Nietzsche at all, the similarities seem to prove otherwise. Chapman and Chapman-Santana analyzed these similarities and found several concepts of Nietzsche that are similar to those of Freud (who published his main works about 30 years after Nietzsche). Their results include the most obvious similarity, the concept of the unconscious mind. Freud believed that the (much bigger) unconscious controls the (much smaller) conscious part of our mind. This idea was already anticipated by Nietzsche (Chapman and Chapman-Santana 1995).

> Nietzsche's analysis of non-egoistic behavior, his proto-Freudian presentation of mental life as driven by processes inaccessible to self-consciousness, and his analysis of the ascetic ideal, ressentiment, and self-deception amount to a picture of human agency, in which all significant aspects of inner experience are 'in reality' desires for the experience of power. (Poellner 2000)

Apart from the concept of the unconscious, Freud seems to also have been inspired by Nietzsche in several others of his theories and concepts, as for example the concept of dreams as *illusions of illusions* and dreaming as a cathartic healing process. Chapman and Chapman-Santana also emphasize that some of the terms used by Freud have originally been coined by Nietzsche.

However, both, Nietzsche and Freud, developed an interest in the irrational side of the human mind. Freud wanted to analyze and understand these irrational parts of the mind in order to find some kind of treatment for them, since he thought them to be a danger for the enlightened, rational European civilization. Freud was deeply embedded in his time and fiercely believed in reason as the only force of progress and development for human beings.

> [R]eason, so Freud felt, is the only tool - or weapon - we have to make sense of life, to dispense with illusions (of which, in Freud's thought, religious tenets are only one), to become independent of fettering authorities, and thus to establish our own authority. ... For him, reason was confined with thought. Feelings and emotions were per se irrational, and hence inferior to thought. (Fromm in Robertson 1995: 113f.)

So he went on to work on his theories of the unconscious mind. "For Freud, the implications of such a discovery were profound: it meant that man's actions are not always rational. And such an idea flew in the face of the ideals of the Enlightenment in no less a way than had Nietzsche's notion that 'God is dead'" (Kreis 2000). According to Robertson, Freud was suffering under this unsolvable dilemma throughout his life - he, a child of the rationalist tradition discovered the unconscious exactly through rational reasoning. But his discovery was so powerful and yet had to be disregarded as inferior.

Much alike Nietzsche, also Freud borrowed the names of Greek gods in order to illustrate his theory. Freud discovered two conflicting principles in human nature, which are expressed as fundamental human desires that are completely opposing each other. The life drive (Eros), that includes and explains sexual desire, and the death drive (Thanatos). Freud used to call these drives at times instincts.

Freud describes the life drive as connected to sexuality, fertility, and creativity. His description of the "id" ("Es"), the unconscious part of the human psyche that acts according to pleasure, seems to have a lot of similarities with Nietzsche's outline of the Dionysian principle.

> The "id" according to Freud, is the home of the instincts. The id constantly demands gratification and in this respect, it is primitive and irrational. The id knows no values, only wants and desires. It has no awareness of good or evil. It demands sexual release and

> the termination of pain. When the id is denied, the individual is frustrated, angry, and unhappy. (Kreis 2000)

The sexual energy described by Freud is "beyond good and evil", it's neutral, simply following its instinctual drive for life.

But Freud's brilliant discoveries were downgraded by this shortsighted restriction to sexuality. His student Carl Gustav Jung built on Freud's theories but broadened the concept of Eros and thus also gave credit to the complexity of human nature that's not only focused on one drive. "For example, a child turns to its mother's breast not merely for food and nourishment, and not merely for oral gratification, but also for love and tenderness" (Robertson 1995: 110). Jung developed Freud's theory on the human unconscious further, but under different auspices: he was convinced that the unconscious was not mainly an individual, but a collective psychic phenomenon. What he could see in the unconscious was not possible for Freud. He would solve Freud's dilemma because he was not so deeply caught in the rationalist school of thought, but open-minded and ready to find what would change the perception of what human beings are. "The way out lay in a synthesis of conscious and unconscious, of mind and body. It lay in relationship, not separation" (Robertson 1995: 114).

I.3 C.G. Jung's concept of the Collective Unconscious

According to Robertson, the analytical psychologist Carl Gustav Jung (1875-1961) saw himself throughout his life as deeply rooted in nature and the environment around him. "He remained faithful all his life to the conviction that the facts of nature are the basis of all knowledge; ... for him nature is not only outside but also within" (von Franz in Robertson 1995: 139). This interconnectedness with nature also predisposed Jung to overcome the gap between science and arts. For his use of language that could be described as poetic although the contents were clearly coming from experimental science, he received extensive criticism from the scientific community. In Robertson's opinion, Jung was one of those rare personalities who managed to bridge the "two cultures of science and the arts" (Robertson 1995: 140). Because of this holistic approach that somehow was part of Jung's character and developed very early in his childhood, Jung was much more ready to accept different possible realities than his colleagues. As Robertson puts it: "He was never able to ignore experience just because it didn't fit his view of reality" (Robertson 1995: 139).

When Jung familiarized himself with the Freudian theory of the unconscious, he was enthusiastically taking it up and thought it would be the solution for his patients as well. But other than the theorist Freud, Jung was a descriptive scientist, and what he observed in his patients didn't at all fit the Freudian theories of the unconscious as just a pool of repressed thoughts and emotions and therefore it came after the conscious. According to his observations, Jung came to the opposite conclusion: that the unconscious was much bigger, stranger, and incomprehensible than the conscious part of the psyche, and that it was there long before the conscious part was developing. Robertson quotes Jung: "(I)n early childhood we are unconscious; the most important functions of an instinctive nature are unconscious, and consciousness is rather the product of the unconscious" (Jung quoted in Robertson 1995: 142).

With this discovery that presented a threat for the scientific dogma that everything that exists in nature can be observed directly once the right methods and tools have been found, Jung couldn't continue to be a disciple of Freud any more. With his concept of the collective unconscious, he separated himself and his scientific work from his colleague and mentor who, in Jung's opinion, failed to recognize the existence of an important part of the human psyche, which is unconsciously sharing a range of human patterns with all other humans beyond time and space limits. Jung calls this common psychological heritage of all humans *archetypes.*

> The collective unconscious is part of the psyche, which can be negatively distinguished from a personal unconscious by the fact that it does not, like the latter, owe its existence to personal experience and consequently is not a personal acquisition. While the personal unconscious is made up essentially of contents that have at one time been conscious but have disappeared from consciousness through having been forgotten or repressed, the contents of the collective unconscious have never been individually acquired, but owe their existence exclusively to heredity. (Jung 2004:1)

Archetypes are representing "[...] die seit Urzeit prävalierenden menschlichen Situationen, das heißt, es gibt Jugend und Alter, Geburt und Tod; es gibt Söhne und Töchter, Väter und Mütter; es gibt Paarung usw. [...]" (Jung 1975: 25. Translation: [...] human situations that are prevalent since primitive times, i.e. there is youth and age, birth and death; there are sons and daughters, fathers and mothers; there is mating etc. [...]).

Archetypes can only be described as empty structures that will be activated if the archetypal situation occurs in a person's life. "The best way to express the situation seems to be that the archetype comes first, but the archetype is empty until the actual experience provides it with the content necessary for expression" (Robertson 1995: 166). As these archetypes are situated in the unconscious part of the human psyche, Jung found out that they are expressed mainly through cultural assets like myths, dreams, arts, music etc. - or, in other words, to stay within the conflict transformation paradigm, through the creative representations of culture. By exploring these cultural fields in different parts of the world, Jung found that many of these symbolic motifs are repeated in different times and at various places.

Jung saw his own theory as a constructive completion of the unconscious how Freud developed it[5]. It is possible to interpret Jung's concept of the unconscious as a kind of positive energy which, due to the fact that it is shared by all humans, can be a source of creativity and empathy, a force of positive transformation.

Even though Jung himself didn't want to claim originality for his concept but rather downplayed the novelty of his findings, his approach can surely be seen as another paradigm shift in European humanistic sciences, and it completely goes against the ruling concept of Western philosophy since Immanuel Kant (1724-1804), which is characterized by the leadership of science-devoted rationality. The newness of Jung's approach is therefore not that he reclaims the existence of archetypal patterns in humanity, so-called universal patterns of human behavior and relations, but that by saying this he challenges the idea of a common human rationality. Because Jung's *archetypes,* or instincts, as he also calls them, are far beyond rationality; they are *trans-rational.*

---

[5] According to a Wikipedia article on C. G. Jung, he saw Freud's concept of the unconscious as too negative as it would only consist of repressed dreams and desires, see http://en.wikipedia.org/wiki/C._G._Jung#The_collective_unconscious. Jung himself saw Freud's and Adler's concepts of the unconscious as incomplete as they saw the psyche of a human being as only personal and individual, and they didn't accept the idea that there is a "second psychic system" (Jung 2004: 1).

The hypothesis of the collective unconscious is, therefore, no more daring than to assume there are instincts. One admits readily that human activity is influenced to a high degree by instincts, quite apart from the rational motivations of the conscious mind."(Jung 2004: 1)

Jung also emphasizes that the archetypes cannot be seen as inherited ideas but they are rather inherited possibilities of ideas (Robertson 1995: 166).

> (T)here are two sides to the archetype: archetypal image and instinctual behavior. Since we experience the world relationally, the archetypes are activated in many, perhaps all, human situations. As we personally experience the world through the archetypes, the archetypes are given a particular, highly personal form. Eventually, the world is almost entirely encountered through our personal memories; the archetypes lie deep within. (Robertson 1995: 168f.)

Robertson understands Jung's theories as an attempt to bring the human being regarding its wholeness back into balance. He sees this wholeness as a balance of the four parts of the human being: body, soul, mind, and spirit. "Wholeness can only be achieved if each of the four parts can harmoniously contain and honor the other three" (Robertson 1995: 208). Additionally, Robertson brings us back to the necessary balance between the Apollonian and the Dionysian principles, when he requests that "(a)n integrated whole demands both control and harmony" (Robertson 1995: 209).

It is not surprising, that this concept was the basis for many scientists who intended to find a way to access and constructively use this great source of human heritage, be it for the benefit of the individual or the collective or, as I would read it, similarly both. Reading Jung in the framework of peace and conflict transformation, it seems to be a unique chance to overcome the dualities and dichotomies that shape our world today, and to reconcile the individual with the collective. Jung's theory can be seen as a source of hope, that there is a way to reach a state of harmony, by exhausting the ever existing relations between the collective and the individual in a mutually supportive manner. For that, it is crucial to learn more about the character and functions of the archetypes and to relate these to the individual and collective actions of all humans.

In the case of conflicts, the archetype theory helps us understand how masses of people can happen to follow an ideology that is as destructive and cruel as the Nazi regime in Germany, argues Jung. For the sake of humankind, it seems, he passionately defends his concept against the Freudian idea of an only individually developing unconscious, when he writes:

> Can we not see how a whole nation is reviving an archaic symbol, yes, even archaic religious forms, and how this mass emotion is influencing and revolutionizing the life of the individual in a catastrophic manner? The man of the past is alive in us today to a degree undreamt of before the war, and in the last analysis, what is the fate of Great nations but a summation of the psychic changes in individuals? (Jung 2004: 2)

This is why we have to study and reveal the archetypes and find out what exactly rests in our collective unconscious, as this is the only chance to reveal what triggers the re-emergence of an archetype with all its positive and negative consequences and concomitants. Like that, we can learn to understand human actions and reactions, and we can for sure learn a lot about conflicts between humans and also about their harmonious relations with each other. In short, it is a way to understand human nature without judging human behavior from the outside and without claiming moral superiority. Only when we realize, what drives our individual or collective actions in different situations, will we be able to transform and transcend these situations in a way that leads us to a more respectful and harmonious conviviality.

Jung explains, how archetypes cannot be understood from any moral and/or rational standpoint, but are just what they are: structures that shape to a certain extent our actions and beliefs, mechanisms of defense and advancement, instincts, if we want, and survival mechanisms that make sure, that not only we as individuals, but also we as members of the human race can know and use what our ancestors learned through all times.

The concept of the collective unconscious and Jung's archetype theory have been extensively criticized for not being consequent and concrete, or in other words, for not being scientific enough. The criticism I found most relevant for the purpose of this book is the sometimes metaphysical, Platonic notion of the archetypes.

Werner Held, for example, writes that it seems as if these are just falling from the sky. He criticizes that Jung doesn't recognize the connectedness between the collective and the individual unconscious, when he insists on the autonomous nature of the archetypes, which have nothing to do with the personal history of the individual.

> Auch wenn vieles für die Existenz kollektiver Bilder spricht, bedeutet das aber nicht, dass ihr Auftauchen nicht in einem festen Sinnzusammenhang von jeweiliger Lebenssituation und frühkindlichen Erfahrungen steht. Jung vernachlässigt diese Zusammenhänge in seiner Faszination für urtümliche Bilder und Mythen fast schon konsequent. (Held 2001. Translation: Although much argues for the existence of collective images, this doesn't mean that their emergence is not connected strongly to a particular life situation and early childhood experiences. In his fascination for pristine images and myths, Jung almost consequently disregards these connections.)

Whether Jung has been misinterpreted by Held or not, the remark seems important as it is exactly our embedding as humans in an environment of different relationships and in different situational backgrounds, or, in other words, our connectedness as much with our actual life world as with the collective unconscious, that predisposes and dynamically directs our actions in either one direction or the other. As Dietrich suggests, the archetypes give a very valuable tool to peace researchers, as they create a space of manifold opportunities for each and every human being. "Jung says that each of us comprises the complete potential to the most horrible deeds of mankind, but at the same time also to the warmest mode of conviviality and solidarity" (Dietrich 2006a: 38).

Jung's approach also stands for the reconciliation of Apollo and Dionysus, and as an acknowledgment that these are just two sides of the same medal.

> Drückt man es allgemein aus, so stehen Form und Energie in einem umgekehrten Verhältnis zueinander: Energie ist das Prinzip der Veränderung, aber eine Form oder Struktur kann nur solange existieren, wie sie einer Veränderung ein gewisses Maß an Stabilität und Widerstand entgegenzusetzen hat. (Jung 1964: 209. Translation: Generally speaking, form and energy are inversely rated to each other: Energy is the principle of change, but a form or a structure can only exist as long as it is able to counter change to a certain degree with stability and resistance.)

This openness of the human condition, which enables each and every one of us to use, for good or bad, the universal knowledge, which exists in another consciousness level, is the fundamental principle of the transpersonal approach (Dietrich 2006a: 39). Deriving from Jung's ideas about the energetics of the psyche, the field of transpersonal psychology and systems philosophy emerged.

I.4 Systems Philosophy: an Interconnected Humanity

Jung understands the human psyche as a system that is fueled by energy. Transpersonal psychology and transrational systemic approaches to conflict transformation have been further developed on the basis of the idea that in a system, all aspects must be recognized just because they are there, depending on and complementing each other.

The biologist Rupert Sheldrake, a leading figure of transpersonal theory and also the maybe most active contributor of scientific experiments to prove theories of the often as pseudo-scientific disregarded field of transpersonal psychology brings another example, which gives us a glimpse of understanding what foundation systemic approaches are built on: on the assumption that there is a collective unconscious that consists of universal patterns of human relations (archetypes) and is shared by every human being. As a scientist, Sheldrake developed Jung's theory further and expanded it from human beings to nature in general. He is convinced that nature itself has a memory, and that what we call natural laws are really no more than habits (Sheldrake 2005).

One important method to prove that archetypes really exist is to collect and compare different spiritual, mythological and cultural representations: Gods and Goddesses, myths, etc. To show that, for instance, Apollo and Dionysus are symbols of two fundamental principles of human existence, Sheldrake introduces two different deities that represent form and energy in a different culture.

> Es gibt also zwei Prinzipien: ein formatives Prinzip, die Felder, und ein energetisches Prinzip. Energie ist das Prinzip der Veränderung, und reine Veränderung wäre Chaos. Eine Möglichkeit, sich diese beiden Prinzipien zu denken, ist die indische tantrische Vorstellung von Shakti als Energie und Shiva als dem formbildenden Prinzip, die in ihrem Zusammenwirken die Welt, wie wir sie kennen, erschaffen. (Sheldrake, McKenna, Abraham 1993: 55. Translation: Thus, there are two principles: a formative principle, the fields, and an energetic principle. Energy

> is the principle of change, and total change would mean chaos. One possibility to think of these two principles is the imagination of the Indian Tantra of Shakti as energy and Shiva as the form-constructing principle that through their cooperation are creating the world as we know it.)

The school of thought of Transpersonal Psychology derived a few decades ago from Jung's concept of the collective unconscious as an area within the discipline of psychology. Lajoie and Shapiro defined transpersonal psychology as the *"study of humanity's highest potential, and with the recognition, understanding, and realization of unitive, spiritual, and transcendent states of consciousness"* (Lajoie and Shapiro, 1992: 91)

Based on Jung's ideas about the energetics of the psyche, where he applies terminologies from physics to the psychological field, the transpersonal psychology approach emerged. Jung understands the human psyche as a system that is fueled by energy, which can be shifted - mostly unconsciously, but also conscious energy shifts are possible - from one part to the other, but can never change its total (Held 2001).

I.4.1 99 and 1 Monkey

The text that is most frequently used to explain what is meant by transpersonal thinking and systems theory is, interestingly, a kind of a fairy tale or myth. This fact as such brings us closer to what these theories want to achieve: a revival of the ancient connection between spirituality and science, between emotions and rationality, between the male and the female principle, between form and energy. The outcomes of its findings therefore are aimed to create *A New Science of Life*, as one of Sheldrake's books is called, or a view of evolution that embraces diversity and creates a holistic picture of the universe and life in general. In other words, it's about overcoming the dualities that came to be fundamental principles of our world view like the duality of form and energy, two principles that have to be essentially united instead of being understood as two opposites. These dualities and oppositions shape our thinking and being in the world, but, and this is what we have to understand with our heart and mind together, they have not always been separated and therefore, a transformation is possible.

> Science became very limited in its focus to mechanical, material things, and religion became very introverted; it became very concerned just with the human spirit and with morality and so

> forth, and so religion signed over the whole of the natural world including the cosmos to science and science signed over to religion human ethical questions and left this terribly limited domain as the sphere of religion. In most traditional cultures, these are not separated in that way. For an American Indian looking at the sky, he's not looking at just a material collection of bodies moving in accordance with inanimate laws. The sky is a living being, the abode of the spirit. The earth is a living mother; it's not just a collection of rocks with physical forces at work in them. So, if you look at any traditional world view there isn't a separation between nature and spirit, and religion and science. The two go together. (Sheldrake 1995/6)

Coming back to the starting point of this chapter, I wanted to go a little bit into the so-called *hundredth monkey phenomenon,* a story about a scientific experiment that proved that even monkeys' evolution happens through accessing something like a collective unconscious or, as Sheldrake calls it with a more scientific term, the *morphic field.* This idea will be elaborated a bit later.

The monkey story was firstly told by Lyann Watson in his book *Lifetide,* but it got a bigger audience through Ken Keyes book *The Hundreth Monkey.* Keyes' version of the story about the monkeys on a Japanese island, that have been observed for over 30 years by scientists, is an impressive document of systemic transpersonal thinking. Scientists provided sweet potatoes to these monkeys, by dropping them in the sand. "The monkeys liked the taste of the raw sweet potatoes, but they found the dirt unpleasant" (Keyes 1981). So, one young monkey found out how to wash the potatoes. She taught her new method to her family and friends. "This cultural innovation was gradually picked up by various monkeys before the eyes of the scientists" (Keyes 1981). He describes how within six years, all young monkeys had learned this new skill. He also observed, that not all adults learned it and that the adults had to be taught by their children in order to get the new skill.

> Then something startling took place. In the autumn of 1958, a certain number of Koshima monkeys were washing sweet potatoes -- the exact number is not known. Let us suppose that when the sun rose one morning there were 99 monkeys on Koshima Island who had learned to wash their sweet potatoes. Let's further

> suppose that later that morning, the hundredth monkey learned to wash potatoes.
>
> THEN IT HAPPENED! By that evening almost everyone in the tribe was washing sweet potatoes before eating them. The added energy of this hundredth monkey somehow created an ideological breakthrough! But notice: A most surprising thing observed by these scientists was that the habit of washing sweet potatoes then jumped over the sea...Colonies of monkeys on other islands and the mainland troop of monkeys at Takasakiyama began washing their sweet potatoes. Thus, when a certain critical number achieves an awareness, this new awareness may be communicated from mind to mind. (Keyes 1981)

Keyes' description obviously tunes perfectly into Sheldrake's transpersonal theories of the morphic field or *morphic resonance.* Keyes even uses the term *field* when he talks about the energy that was created by the 100th monkey and that lead to the transmission of a new awareness. This is a story about social change, meant as an encouragement for people during the Cold War to start acting and influencing others instead of backing down convinced that "as a single person I anyways can't change anything". The story definitely has an empowering aspect to it since it makes us aware of the fact that each and every individual is important, and everyone of us could be the crucial one, the one hundredth monkey that helps the group reach a critical point after which everybody will join.

Sheldrake's theory of the morphic field challenges the so far mostly unquestioned *big bang theory,* which he considers highly unprovable and not very likely. As we can see, the universe is developing and changing all the time, he states. From that point of view, it is not very likely that there are natural laws which have always been there and will always be true. He thus challenges another basis for our (Apollonian) civilization: The eternal form, on which we build our natural sciences that replaced God as an eternal, one and only truth, is not eternal, but changeable. As we see, the laws that we call the laws of nature still seem to stay the same for a long, long time. Sheldrake explains this with the thesis that the universe works on the ground of habituation. Consequently, he suggests talking about "natural habits" instead of "natural laws".

> Die Regelmäßigkeiten der Natur sind habitueller Art. Die Dinge sind, wie sie sind, weil sie waren, wie sie waren. Das Universum ist ein in ständiger Entwicklung begriffenes System von

> Gewohnheiten. (Sheldrake, McKenna, Abraham 1993: 20. Translation: The regularities of nature are habitual. Things are how they are, because they were how they were. The universe is a constantly changing system of habits.)

The transmission of these natural habits works somehow like Jung's collective unconscious, assumes Sheldrake. He is working for decades to provide empirical evidence for this theory, and he seems to be successful, when he proves that rats can learn the same trick faster and faster over generations, and not only that: it not only works through time, but also through space; once rats in the US learned something new over fifteen generations, their fellows in Australia start with their first generation where the US rats' 15th generation stopped.

The explanation for these phenomena is the *morphic field* theory that Sheldrake developed: this field that exists next to other fields like magnetic fields contains the memories of the whole universe, and these memories can be accessed. Other than Jung's theory of the collective unconscious or Stanislaw Grow's theory of the *phylogenetic unconscious,* who assumed that the memories of all times and places are transmitted through the genes from one generation to the other, proved Sheldrake that the morphic field exists beyond any material basis (Held 2001).

If morphic fields are form-creating fields, i.e. fields that lead to the habitual re-creation of forms, by using and applying the acquired knowledge out of experiences, the question remains, how new forms can be created. The link between form and energy, or transcendent creativity, is easy to detect.

Also Sheldrake and his colleague Terence McKenna realize humanity's loss, when the ancient way of life, where Apollo and Dionysus were allowed to live, create and re-create side by side, got replaced by a new paradigm, which was much less dynamic and energetic, and hence led to the development of the egocentric self, as McKenna puts it. (Sheldrake, McKenna, Abraham 1993: 86ff) With the introduction of a male, singular God and the abandoning of the Great Mother, and all her Gods and Goddesses, our individualistic, competition-oriented society came into being. McKenna connects this development with the male principle, the ordering principle, that condemns the principle of free flowing, uncontrollable energies - a principle that he connects with the female, as the female has by nature more border-experiences in her life (i.e. the birth of her children) than the male.

Riane Eisler (The Chalice and the Blade, 1988) went beyond the limiting male-female duality and suggested the transition from a partnership-oriented into a power-oriented society. She gets support from renowned system theorists like the mathematician and chaos theorist Ralph Abraham, who says that "the repression of chaos began with the patriarchal takeover six thousand years ago" (Abraham 1997).

Before ending this chapter, I want to introduce Elaine Myers critique of Keyes' version in her short article *The Hundredth Monkey Revisited* (1985) for having "invented" the crucial part of it. Although Keyes declares the story a"legend" right from the beginning and obviously uses it for the purpose of empowering individuals to act for social change, she argues that the original story as Watson wrote it would have been more realistic and in the same way encouraging.

> In the original reports, there was no mention of the group passing a critical threshold that would impart the idea to the entire troop. The older monkeys remained steadfastly ignorant of the new behavior. Likewise, there was no mention of widespread sweet potato washing in other monkey troops. (Myers 1985: 10)

But for Myers, these are not bad news at all. She almost seems to refuse the need to explain systemic processes like information transmission with highly scientific hypotheses like Sheldrake's field theories. She doesn't state whether these theories are probable or not, but insists on the fact that in the case of the monkeys, there is no proof for their accuracy. The really impressive findings about how human evolution works are, to her, obvious in the story and they don't need scientific measure. With her emphasis on the fact that evolutionary development in the case of the Koshima monkeys worked through direct communication and cooperation she anticipates current findings in neurobiology, which will be elaborated in chapter I.4.3. To understand how successful social transformation movements might build up their transformative potential, Meyers' conclusion of the 100th monkey story is very convincing for me personally, as it encourages becoming active for change:

> What this research does suggest, however, is that holding positive ideas (as important a step as this is) is not sufficient by itself to change the world. We still need direct communication between individuals, we need to translate our ideas into action, and we need to recognize the freedom of choice of those who choose alternatives different from our own. (Myers 1985: 10)

I.4.2 The World as an Interconnected System

The idea to see the universe as an organized system of "interrelated subsystems" (Boulding K. 1994: 26) lies at the bottom of systems thinking. As a matter of fact, biology sees the human organism as a complex system *(biosystem)* and illnesses as a sign that the intrasystemic balance is not in place. Consequently, biology was one of the first disciplines to introduce systemic approaches. Soon enough, the idea was born to develop a *general system theory* as an interdisciplinary project that would help understand systems of all kinds and forms (von Bertalanffy in Laszlo 1972: xvii).

Kenneth Boulding provides us with a very broad definition of a system as "anything that is not chaos" or, turning this statement around, "any structure that exhibits order and pattern" (Boulding K. 1985: 9). According to Boulding, there are three major types of systems in the world: *physical systems, biological systems, and social systems.* These three types of systems correspond to levels of complexity and they developed in the above chronological order. It also says something about their stability: physical systems are more stable (predictable) than biological systems than social systems. But since our current social system is influencing to a great degree the biological and physical systems of the earth, also these systems become less and less predictable (for example, think about the relationship between greenhouse gases and global warming or other social-physical system relationships) (Boulding K. 1994 45ff; Boulding K. 1985 31f). The effects of the social systems' emissions into the biosphere, for instance, are unpredictable, although we are quite sure that there is an interconnection and thus, there will be an effect.

System theory is based on the assumption that seeing the full picture, acknowledging the structures and patterns of a system as a whole is important for any kind of scientific analysis. This was a new way of seeing, since the traditional scientific approach was based on the analysis of particular parts and pieces of whatever system. But system theory assumes that the interconnections of the different parts of a system are as important to understand how the system works as are the parts themselves. Furthermore, system theory aims at detecting the common characteristics of systems, no matter how different they might be. Ludwig von Bertalanffy (1901-1972), an Austrian biologist, one of the pioneers of general system theory, states: "Modern technology and society have become so complex that traditional ways and means are not sufficient anymore - approaches of a 'holistic' (or systems) and generalist nature have to be introduced" (van

Bertalanffy in Laszlo 1972: xviii). Ervin Laszlo, a Hungarian system theorist uses a more drastic language when he emphasizes the need for an integral philosophy based on systems thinking:

> We appear to be part of an interconnected system of nature, and unless informed 'generalists' make it their business to develop systematic theories of the patterns of interconnection, our short-range projects and limited control-abilities may lead us to our own destruction. (Laszlo 1972: 4)

Laszlo criticizes the scientific strive for more and more specialized knowledge, the mania to analyze the integral parts of the universe into smaller and smaller units, while there is no serious attempt to understand the universe as a whole. He argues that the "facts" they produce as separated specialists have no relevance for human concern (Laszlo 1972: 6). The escape from the notion of a more and more meaningless life into religious and spiritual movements is a direct consequence of the complete failure of modern science to give answers for pressing problems of humans all over the world. The human desire for wholeness and connectedness (or, as we could say: our desire for the Dionysian in our life) thus cannot be fulfilled, and the consequence is a complete lack of motivation and meaning in the western world, where basic needs are fulfilled and no other action is required to guarantee the physical survival. "Specialized science is simply irrelevant to the question of meaning in life" (Laszlo 1972: 6f). This is why he warns in such a drastic tone of our "destruction" - because this apathy and lack of orientation in our life might be deadly in the end, since there are pressing problems (environmental, developmental, economic etc.) that would need our immediate attention, our creativity, empathy and action.

Coming back to the characteristics of each system that may exist, Laszlo starts his considerations from the commonplace "the whole is more than the sum of its parts", that found entrance into our general knowledge. This saying though in a slightly different version, which goes "wholes [...] are *other* than the sum of their parts" (Laszlo 1972: 37) shows mathematical evidence.

> The noteworthy point for our consideration is that the mathematics of non-summative complexes applies to physical, biological, psychological, as well as sociological systems. These systems form ordered wholes, i.e., constitutive complexes, in which the law-bound regularities exhibited by interdependent elements

> determine the functional behavior of the totality. (Laszlo 1972: 37f)

In simpler terms, we can say with Laszlo that the "behavior" of a total system depends not only on the "behavior" of all its parts, but also and in particular on the relationships between the single elements.

As a consequence of the findings of systems philosophy, Laszlo sees humanity today at a cross-road, a so-called *bifurcation point*[6]. He emphasizes the importance of ideas and visions, and according to systems philosophy, the right ideas, once they are "born", will spread and affect people. Robertson, too, believes in the emergence of what he calls *Great Theories,* big changes in world view, at the right time and he connects their appearance with a sufficient energy buildup in a society. "Great Theories reflect the *Zeitgeist.* Most often, a great theory develops because there is a need for such a theory. If the need is not great enough, the energy to produce such a massive rethinking of reality is just not present" (Robertson 1995: 26). Laszlo argues that world views and ideas about human nature are guiding any kind of social change, "especially when traditional modes of thought and patterns of behavior break down" (Laszlo 1972: 281). Utopian visions about a better society where values like justice, equality and non-discrimination are leading can therefore enhance these transformation processes and make the unrealistic real, at least until the transformation process itself has come to an end.

K. Boulding adds an important proposition to this by asking why we want to analyze systems: Because we want to make statements about the future that are somehow probable. In his essay, *The Range of Possible Futures,* he understands systems thinking as one way to figure out which possible futures we can imagine which, again, is a starting point for our future decisions. We could also say systems analysis tries to prevent us from repeating the mistakes of the past. "All decisions involve choices among

---

[6] I am using the term "bifurcation point" as it is used in general systems theory. A functional definition would be:

In mathematics, specifically in the study of dynamical systems, a bifurcation occurs when a small smooth change made to the parameter values (the bifurcation parameters) of a system causes a sudden 'qualitative' or topological change in the system's long-term dynamical behavior

(http://www.answers.com/topic/bifurcation-theory-1?cat=technology)

images of possible futures. How we get these images, therefore, and how accurate they are, is a crucial problem in what might be called the theory of bad decisions; that is, how do we avoid decisions that we later regret?" (Boulding K.1995: 39). At the same time, the idea that human decisions determine the future is also the main differentiating factor between the sociosphere and the biosphere. (Boulding K. 1985: 82)

Laszlo divides the different stages after system change into the *stabilization* stage and after that (after the dust calms down) the *organization* stage. Social systems are, according to this theory, "capable of both self-stabilization and self-*organization*" (Laszlo 1972: 106).

Kenneth Boulding emphasizes that for analyzing social systems, we have to understand the nature of human interactions. He distinguishes three fundamental kinds of interactions: threats, exchange, and love. All interactions are a combination of these three types. (Boulding K. 1995: 47)

To get to a deeper understanding of the energetic processes in a social system, K. Boulding's identification of the three principles of social systems is very helpful:

The first one is the **General Law of Conservation:** "[...] if there is a fixed quantity of anything, it can be pushed around only among subsystems, so that growth in any subsystem must involve decline in all the others taken together." (Boulding K. 1995: 33; 1985: 16) This principle though has on our planet been weakened by the fact that the continuous evolution of new genetic know-how is modifying the "fixed quantity of anything" continuously. For example non-renewable resources: since there are ever new sources discovered, the complexity of the system limits the applicability of the law of conservation.

The second principle is what Boulding calls **the Generalized Second Law**[7]: "[...] if anything happens, it is because there is a potential for its happening, and after it has happened, that potential has been used up." (Boulding K. 1995: 33; 1985: 16)

The third principle is the **Recreation Potential of Potentials:** "The key here is that evolutionary systems are dominated by information and know-

7 The Second Law of Thermodynamics or entropy can be summarized with the following definition: Entropy is "(t)he energy form of a system that relates to its internal state of disorder. High entropy levels are disordered states, low entropy levels are characteristic of ordered states." (http://www.whatislife.com/glossary/e.htm)

how structures, and information is not conserved, as everyone who teaches a class knows. At the end of the class, frequently the students know more and so does the teacher." (Boulding K. 1995: 34)

Laszlo elaborates the characterization of politically organized societies (in the sense of a society organized as a nation-state) further and distinguishes two exogenous impetuses for society transformation: national and international pressures, "provided the national pressures come from the individuals and the culture-system, and not from within the social system and its institutions." (Laszlo 1972: 106f) According to Boulding, these "pressures" again will consist of all three kinds of human interactions: they will include threats, without doubt, but also exchange (economy, for example) and love (and hate) aspects (Boulding K. 1995: 47).

This is an important addition that should be kept in mind for the application of the theories in the second part of this book, the case study on the Nicaraguan revolution. For this case, it is also helpful to take a closer look at Laszlo's ideas about the internal hierarchy of social systems. As the ones who make paradigm shifts in a society possible by packing the energy potentials into a new great theory, he attributes special importance to decision makers and opinion leaders. The model he suggests to explain the process of social change has to do with the hierarchy that is inherent to social systems: "At the top controlling level of the hierarchy of a social system, change affects the paramount value system, and from here it radiates to progressively lower levels, until it reaches the role-level of the individual, affecting his behavior and motivation." (Laszlo 1972: 108) The importance of a balance in the power relations of the social system, in a traditionally patriarchal system especially in the gender relations, will be elaborated later. But as a side note I would like to mention it - just to make clear, that the affection of the behavior and motivation of "the individual" in the sense of a majority of individuals in a society (which is necessary for the long-ranging transformation of a society) highly depends on the non-discriminatory recognition of (ideally) every individual, or at least every significant group of individuals that constitute the mentioned society, regardless of sex, age, social class, ethic group, race, etc.

The Dionysian aspect in this description is quite obvious: since it was the archaic Dionysian ritual, where all kinds of social hierarchies based on different attributes were suspended for a while, a situation that supported the spirit of community and cooperation. It is such a situation where the commonalities are put forth and the things that separate different groups and individuals from each other don't happen, since the common goal is in the forefront, that can make change happen, argues also Laszlo.

Neurobiology has an answer to the question, why such collective experiences are so intense and mean so much to us.

I.4.3 The human organism as a system based on cooperation

One of the most complex systems that exist is the human body. Since Charles Darwin (1809-1882), we know that biological evolution means the development of more and more complex (organic) systems, from the earliest protoorganisms to the most complex of species, the human being. An evolutionary transformation takes place within the gene pool of a specific species and its effects can be seen only after many generations. Variation and selection is the basis for system transformation into more complex systems. The main question for biologists and geneticists is and was: what is the motivation for an organism to develop onto a different complexity level? Speaking with Ervin Laszlo, we could also ask, what marks the bifurcation point when the evolutionary development produced a differentiation, which is the term Laszlo prefers for being more precise than complexity (Laszlo 1972: 108), i.e., one species' split up into different species?

In a recent publication, *Prinzip Menschlichkeit* (2006) the German medical doctor and psychotherapist Joachim Bauer elaborated a thorough analysis of recent neurobiological data that leads us to a completely different view on human nature than the one Darwin's heritage left us with. Instead of competition and fighting against each other, our organism is really oriented towards cooperation, Bauer states and his arguments are based on solid scientific facts.

Our current view on human nature basically derives from Darwinism, explains Bauer. The key terms in Darwin's theory of evolution are the *struggle for life* and the *war of nature.* Evolution therefore would be based on the survival of the fittest, and the elimination of weaker elements. From Darwin's theories, a scientific discipline called "sociobiology" derived. Its main proponent, Wilson Dawkins, published his main work in 1975, called *The selfish gene.* In this paradigm, even altruistic behavior becomes just disguised selfishness (Loye 2004a: 10). Since then, the idea that even genes are participating in the Darwinist *struggle for life* and fight against other genes for their own survival and multiplication became some kind of "general knowledge" in our society, although it is, according to Bauer, not proven by any facts. But since our societal order was already oriented towards economic competition and material growth, it embraced these ideas that seemed to confirm what humans all over the world were experiencing.

K. Boulding criticizes Darwin for having used "inappropriate metaphors" when he wrote about the *survival of the fittest* and *struggle for life.* He suggests to use survival of the fitting instead, thus emphasizing the question, "fit for what"? The answer can only be "for survival", he argues, which is why the phrase doesn't mean anything.

> The crude kind of 'social Darwinism' that identifies fitness with toughness and competitiveness is a gross misunderstanding of the complexities of the system. The survival strategies in ecological interaction are very diverse. They consist of finding a niche - that is, fitting into the system. (Boulding K. 1985: 65)

Also the other well-known metaphor, *struggle for existence,* is a rather unfortunate phrasing, since there would be only very little struggle to see in our planet's biosphere. "Biological evolution, then, is a profoundly nondialectical process. It does not proceed by any kind of conscious struggle or by winning fights. It proceeds by "differential patterns of adaptability to changing environments" (Boulding K. 1985: 65).

David Loye and his colleagues from *The Darwin Project* present a different view on Darwin's teachings. They agree with Bauer about his essential statement that the human being is focused on cooperation instead of competition, but they don't see Darwin as proposing this misleading view. Instead, Loye writes about the "lost half" of Darwin's theory of evolution. In reality, he states, Darwin himself identified love and moral sensitivity as the prime drives for human evolution (Loye 2004a: 1). In his book *The Great Adventure. Towards a Fully Human Theory of Evolution* (2004), Loye advocates a new view on Darwin's theories, for the sake of humanity and the survival of our planet. He starts off with some surprising quantitative data:

> Today, the focus is mainly on Darwin's *Origin of Species.* But in the 828 page sequel in which he tells us he will now deal with *human* evolution, *The Descent of Man,* Darwin writes only *twice* of "survival of the fittest," but *95 times of love.* He writes of selfishness 12 times, but *92 times of moral sensitivity.* Of competition 9 times, but *24 times of mutuality and mutual aid.* And of what so often

> everywhere today seems to be missing in global political, economic, and religious leadership — that is, of *mind* and *brain* — he writes *200 times.* (Loye 2004b: 3)

In search for the "better story", i.e. a story about human evolution and human nature that would give new perspectives and bring an optimistic message about our future to today's world's citizens, Loye especially focuses on Darwin's own story in the book *The Descent of Man* (1871), a publication that's intended to explain human evolution in particular. In this book, Darwin writes of human values that through evolution came to play a much more important role than the struggle for existence:

> Important as the struggle for existence has been and even still is, yet as far as the highest part of man's nature is concerned, there are other agencies more important. For the moral qualities are advanced, either directly or indirectly, much more through the effects of habit, the reasoning powers, instruction, religion, etc., than through natural selection; though to this latter agency may be safely attributed the social instincts, which afforded the basis for the development of the moral sense. (Darwin 1871)

According to neurobiological data, the assumption that genes are fighting against each other is wrong, as is the assumption that competition and struggle are the inherent driving forces of humanity. Lynn Margulis, a famous US-American biologist, emphasizes that terms like "competition" and "struggle for life" are taken from business-language and are not genuine biological terms. Biology doesn't know success-oriented thought structures as economy does (Bauer 2006: 18f).

On the other hand, not only humans and all other mammals are oriented towards cooperation and resonance, but the general structure of the universe favors cooperation, we could say. As Kenneth Boulding states,

> Two species, **A** and **B**, have a cooperative relationship if the more of **A**, the more of **B**, and the more of **B**, the more of **A**. This is much more common in the biosphere than is sometimes thought. The tooth and claw may be visible, but the invisible helping hand may be much more significant in the long run. (Boulding K. 1985: 40)

To imagine that the world and its different systems developed into the miraculous diversity that it is today on the basis of competition and fight seems indeed very unlikely, if we look at the effects that war and violence has on human societies - it seems obvious that wars generally move us rather backward than forward in the evolutionary process. Even between the main systems of the world, cooperative exchange cycles are necessary. K. Boulding brings examples like the nitrogen cycle[8] or the oxygen/carbon dioxide cycle[9].

Following this general rule of exchange and cooperation in the world, the core motivation of all our human activities is to get recognition, acceptance, care, and affection (Bauer 2006: 21). As proof for this revolutionary thought he explains how motivation systems/ reward systems (messenger substances inherent to the human body that work like drugs) are released in order to achieve the main aim of human motivation, that is: social community and successful relationships. All every-day-goals of human activity - be it financial, professional or material goals - follow this higher goal of being socially recognized and, furthermore, being loved. (Bauer 2006: 34ff)

I.4.3.1 "Die stärkste und beste Droge für den Menschen ist der andere Mensch"

(Bauer 2006: 52. Translation: The strongest and best drug for a human being is the other human being). This statement turns our common view of human nature upside down. But since we are observing a lot of violations of this principle every day, Bauer emphasizes another principle: genetic potentials are like tools that have to be used in order to have an effect. If we don't use our potentials, they will get deactivated and so they will be lost for us. And here, an old finding of psychology comes in, that tells us that children who make negative interpersonal experiences from early childhood to youth will have limited relationship ability in their later life. And since very young children are dependent on others, they are also dependent on the fact that good relationship experiences will be given to

---

[8] Bacteria take nitrogen from the atmosphere, give it to plants, they turn it into proteins, give those to animals that eat the plant, there it is turned into more complex proteins, until the animal excretes it for immediate use of plants or dies and gives it to the atmosphere again. (Boulding K. 1985: 40)

[9] Plants take in CO_2 in the sunlight, and then give out oxygen after the process of photosynthesis, that will be breathed in by animals who breathe out CO_2. (Boulding K. 2985: 40) We could say that animals could not have arisen without the "help" of plants.

them. "Mangelnde Zuwendung in der Frühphase der Entwicklung eines Menschen beschädigt die Motivationssysteme des Körpers" (Bauer 2006: 54. Translation: A lack of care in the early stages of human development is harming the motivation systems of the body).

The system of the so-called "mirror cells" (Spiegelnervenzellen) is another proof for the orientation of the human organism towards resonance and reflection: these cells are responsible for the possibility to feel another person's feelings, to experience pain or happiness for and with somebody else. The ability to sympathy and empathy is based in these cells. But we can also observe that some people have a greater ability to be empathic than others, and this again depends on good relationship experiences in our childhood (Bauer 2006: 71).

I.4.3.2 The role of aggression

What role does aggression play in this new view on human nature? Bauer states that even aggression is in the service of relationships. More concretely, we become aggressive when we feel a need to defend a relationship or our social standing, or when we feel that there is a potential of losing an important relationship in our life. Neurobiological experiments showed a correlation between distrust and aggression: when we feel that we are not trustworthy, our aggression level rises. "Vertrauen schafft Vertrauen. Misstrauen und Ablehnung begünstigen Aggression" (Bauer 2006: 75. Translation: Trust creates trust. Distrust and rejection favor aggression). This perspective on aggression again turns our understanding of human nature upside down. "If you can't beat them, join them", one of the key sayings in the Anglo-Saxon world, turns into "If you can't join them, beat them" - an experience which many of us will recognize, at least if we think of childhood and school relationships and what happens if a child gets rejected and disregarded.

Again, neurobiology found a proof for this insight: Through experiments, scientists found out that our brain doesn't make any significant difference between *physical pain* and *social pain* (Bauer 2006: 78f).

An experiment with baby monkeys taken away from their mothers and given to other mothers, some of them showing aggressive behavior, some not, proved that aggressive behavior is by no means transmitted genetically. This experiment proves that aggressive behavior is socially learned and not genetically determined, and it supports neurobiological findings of the genetic potentials for cooperation and care within humans, whose use depends on the early childhood relationship experiences of every single individual.

As this experiment proves that aggression is a learned and not an inherited attitude, in the same way as our childhood experiences enable or limit/disable our ability to cooperation and love, was also Darwin already emphasizing the high importance of education and mutual learning (Loye 2004a).

Also systems theorists realized soon that the human being developed into a creature that functions differently from all other creatures. We could also say that processes of education and learning have replaced biological evolution. The scientific term for this phenomenon is *Noogenetics:* "It is the development of learned structures in nervous systems or their equivalent that are then transmitted from one generation to the next by a learning process" (Boulding K. 1995: 27). He calls the transition from biogenetic to noogenetic evolution fundamental. Noogenetic evolution doesn't only take place for the human race, although the potential for noogenetic evolution that has been prepared by biogenetics "can be realized only if there is a learning process in the course of life of the organism" (Boulding 1985: 66). As an example for proven noogenetic processes in other organisms than human beings, Boulding uses our famous hundredth monkey story. The episode of monkeys teaching a newly learned skill to their fellows and finally, the knowledge transmission jumps from one generation to the other is an excellent example for "substantial changes in behavior without any change whatever, as far as it is known, in the biogenetic structure" (Boulding K. 1985: 66).

In the case of human beings, however, noogenetic evolution became the almost exclusive way of evolution for the last 50.000 years. The consequence of noogenetics is, once again, that human decisions are to a large extent determining the future and fate of our whole planet and also of every subsystem. It is of crucial importance to understand that human learning as a complex multilevel process is the main factor for every kind of social change. (Boulding K. 1985: 83)

I.4.3.3 Preconditions for a successful relationship

Another important factor for Bauer is that certain game theory experiments also prove rational-choice-theory wrong. He mentions, among others, the example of a situation where a person gets a certain amount of money (10 US Dollars, for example), and has to offer whatever he/she considers a fair share of this amount to a second player. The second player can accept or decline the offer. If the offer is accepted, both players can take the money home, if the second player declines the offer, the money is lost for both or reduced by half and the game has to start again. Both players know all the rules beforehand. Rational choice theory would suggest that the second player accepts any amount of money since it's rational to take even a smaller amount of money than to get nothing, but the outcome of the experiment proves that offers that are not considered fair by the second player are turned down frequently (actually, only 50:50 deals get accepted always; 60:40 gets accepted by a majority still but 70:30 or 80:20 deals get rejected most of the time). Why are people rather turning down any offer of money instead of accepting whatever is more than nothing? The clue lies in our desire to be trusted and to trust in others, and to have good and functioning relationships. Fair arrangements are important for having good relationships, whereas being cheated or treated in an unfair way can cause aggression.

Bauer identifies five preconditions for successful relations that provide a good summary of his theory:

1. To see and to be seen (in the sense of being recognized as a person)
2. Mutual attention
3. Emotional resonance
4. Acting together
5. Understanding motives and intentions (Bauer 2006: 190-193)

Finally, Bauer appeals for a societal structure based on cooperation, since it could be scientifically proven that human beings are not made for fight and selection. A society based on cooperation can develop strategies for all the daily challenges it faces, and these strategies can be developed through dialog and cooperation. He doesn't talk about a utopian world where economy is not important at all, but he argues against the neo-liberal notion that sees economic competitiveness as the end-goal of society (Bauer 2006: 202-203).

The argument for cooperation and successful relationships is convincing enough: as neurobiology can prove, they result in greater motivation, and motivation is a very valuable attitude also in the economic world. But motivation is also a crucial attitude for every attempt to transform societies. Especially transformations that need a big amount of energy are highly dependent on motivated people who are ready to give their best for the common goal. The expression "the common goal" already suggests that the existence of cooperation and resonance has been an important contribution to the successful revolution in Nicaragua in 1979.

Like the need for relationships and social life, are processes of cultural creativity too reflection- and resonance phenomena. Bauer mentions here creative processes like painting, joint movement (like dancing) and, above all, all forms of music. He concludes:

> Kulturelle Kreativität ist keineswegs ein Luxusphänomen, sondern Ausdruck der Suche nach dem, worauf wir unserem tiefsten biologischen Wesen nach ausgerichtet sind- (Bauer 2006: 223. Translation: Cultural creativity is by no means a luxury phenomenon, but the expression of the search for that, towards what we are oriented from our deepest biological nature).

I.5 Cultures of Peace(s). Partnership versus Dominance

In this chapter, I want to examine the possibilities for a future that is not based on the patriarchal order of things or, as Riane Eisler puts it, the dominator-model of society. In her book *The Chalice and the Blade. Our History, Our Future* (1988), Eisler calls this alternative societal order the *partnership-model.* Her theories are relevant for this book insofar as the main objective of her research, that tends to prove the existence of such partnership-oriented societies in our history and prehistory, is to prove that the transformation of the dominant societal order in today's world is a real possibility rather than a utopian idea. Thus, Eisler calls her theory the *Cultural Transformation Theory (CTT).* As we will further see in this chapter, by using Eisler's terminology, we could interpret the Nicaraguan revolution as an attempt to transform a dominator-society into a partnership-society. The questions that will be raised in the following case-study, by analyzing "what went wrong" in Nicaragua from a(n) (intra-)systemic perspective that evaluates the transformation processes in Nicaraguan society, mainly focus on the question, how (by what means) this cultural transformation could (ideally) take place.

I believe that Eisler herself would definitely consider the Nicaraguan revolution as one attempt to transform culture into a partnership society, when she states:

> The larger picture that emerges indicates that all the modern, post-Enlightenment movements for social justice, be they religious or secular, as well as the more recent feminist, peace, and ecology movements, are part of an underlying thrust for the transformation of a dominator to a partnership system. (Eisler 1988: xx)

CTT seeks to overcome the male domination of history and tries to develop a holistic, or systemic, perspective of humanity as a whole. Instead of splitting humanity in two halves, men and women, according to biology, and thus attributing different attitudes to each of these two halves, CTT acknowledges that another organization model for societies is possible by taking into account examples of societal structures, in prehistory, history and our present times, that are based on partnership and care for each other instead of hierarchy and domination. These examples, where men contribute and commit themselves to the partnership-orientation of their society demonstrate that men are not essentially prone to be dominators.

Eisler defines cultures that belong to the dominator-paradigm as not only (and not essentially) male-dominated, but these cultures "also have a generally hierarchic and authoritarian social structure and a high degree of social violence, particularly warfare" (Eisler 1988: xix).

I.5.1 The Time of the Great Mother

Riane Eisler goes conform to the analysis of systems philosophers like Ervin Laszlo that the world is at a cross-roads today, at a crucial bifurcation point in history. With her theory, she hopes to contribute that instead of a system breakdown, a breakthrough will be at the end of this. As has already been mentioned in Chapter I, the starting point of Eisler's analysis is the fact that for thousands of years in the Neolithic period, when the first agrarian settlements were founded and communities developed, and even already before that, a mother goddess was the most important deity, worshiped in all known early agrarian societies. "We find evidence of the deification of the female - who in her biological character gives birth and nourishment just as the earth does - in the three main centers for the origins of agriculture: Asia Minor and southeastern Europe, Thailand in Southeast Asia, and later on also Middle America" (Eisler 1988: 21).

Eisler discovered that Neolithic art from Goddess-worshiping societies doesn't show war scenes or scenes of slavery, no heroic warrior motives etc. Instead, the most depicted motives are motives that worship and praise nature, a fact that demonstrates the strong connection between the great Goddess and nature.

> Indeed, this theme of unity of all things in nature, as personified by the Goddess, seems to permeate Neolithic art. For here, the supreme power governing the universe is a divine Mother who gives her people life, provides them with material and spiritual nurturance, and who even in death can be counted on to take her children back into her cosmic womb. (Eisler 1988: 19)

Eisler stresses that the automatic assumption that, if there was no patriarchy, there must have been matriarchy (as a system where women dominate men), cannot be proven by any evidence but rather seems to be a projection of our own internalized conceptual framework, the one we grew up with and perceive as "natural". The dichotomized world-view based on "either/or" narrows our view and our imagination. The evidence suggests otherwise:

> Analogizing from this different conceptual framework, we can see that the fact that women played a central and vigorous role in prehistoric religion and life does not have to mean that men were perceived and treated as subservient. For here, both men and women were the children of the Goddess, as they were the children of the women who headed the families and clans. And while this certainly gave women a great deal of power, analogizing from our present-day mother-child relationship, it seems to have been a power that was more equated with responsibility and love than with oppression, privilege, and fear. (Eisler 1988: 28)

Reading this quote in the framework of Kenneth Boulding's system theory, according to which there are three types of relational systems prevalent in the social system, it would mean that in these early societies, the *integrative system,* e.g. the one that includes love and hate, was much more in the foreground than the threat system, on which our current world order is mainly based. This mention seems important to me to show that the early agrarian peoples that lived as children of the Great Mother were not utopian in the sense of unreachable and perfect[10]. As we see in Boulding,

---

[10] See also the concept of imperfect peace of the Spanish peace researcher Francisco Munoz: "From any perspective, peace should not be considered as "total", closed, the endpoint, an almost impossible to achieve "utopian" goal,

the social system is always a combination of all three subsystems. In Eisler's words: "None of this is to say that these societies were ideal. [...] It is important to stress that a peaceful society does not signify the absence of all violence; that these were societies made up of flesh and blood human beings, with human foibles and failings" (Eisler 1988:74).

The fatal shift from the early partnership-oriented societies in the Neolithic period to the ruling societal model of today, the dominator-model, started about 7000 years ago, explains Eisler, with the invasion and expansion of nomadic warrior peoples and supported by several natural catastrophes that brought the cultural evolution to a standstill: the Indo-European tribes that conquered the Indian subcontinent and Europe, and the Semitic tribes that conquered the Old Testament's "holy land", Canaan. This also marks the complete change in spirituality from a polytheistic to a monotheistic religious orientation; a change that took place through conquest and force (Eisler 1988: 44f). From now on, society was structured by a male-dominated hierarchy (introducing social inequality i.e. tribe leaders accumulating the communities' wealth), and an authoritarian and violent leadership. Another difference to their forerunners was "the way they characteristically acquired material wealth [...] not by developing technologies of production, but through ever more effective technologies of destruction" (Eisler 1988: 45). This is when the "sharp blade" became the symbol of civilization.

I.5.1.1 The Crete Phenomenon

The most famous archaeological site that pictures a culture that was evidently different from all dominator-oriented societies we know is Minoan Crete: the artifacts show a society that was based on aesthetics and arts, on the comfortable life; an equitable society where everybody got enough and nobody was poor; a culture where for 1500 years (!) there was no war. Although the Cretans had weapons and might even have had to fight sea-fights to defend themselves, there is no sign of an idealization of warfare. The love of life was prevailing and a strong connection to nature could be proved (see Eisler 1988: 29ff). In Crete, responsibility (a perception connected with motherhood) was the fundamental principle of power, not obedience (as response to force or fear of force) as what we see

---

except at great expense unrealistic and, consequently, frustrating, but as counterproductive inasmuch as it can be the source of violence." (Munoz 2005: 29)

power based on in the current dominator paradigm. With the example of Crete we can also prove, that hierarchy and warfare do not naturally emerge with the development of more complex political structures i.e. the state.

> The assertion that the city-state, or what some modern scholars call 'statism', structurally requires warfare, hierarchism, and the subjugation of women is thus not borne out. In the city-states of Crete, legendary for their wealth, superb arts and crafts, and flourishing trade, it is notable that new technologies, and with them a larger and more complex scale of social organization including increasing specialization, did not bring about any deterioration in the status of women." (Eisler 1988: 38)

The Cretan artifacts also suggest a more natural and liberal acting out of sexuality, a behavior that fits perfectly to the general attitude of enjoying life and its pleasures in the Cretan society. This seems to have been an important contribution to the partnership-orientation of the society, since the societal (religious, moral or political) restrictions on sexual freedom usually contribute on a smaller or bigger scale to the predominant gender inequalities in the respected societies. "Along with their enthusiasm for sports and dancing and their creativity and love for life, these liberated attitudes toward sex seem to have contributed to the generally peaceful and harmonious spirit predominant in Cretan life" (Eisler 1988: 39).

I.5.1.2 System stability and system change

To understand what happened in our past when the partnership paradigm was replaced with the dominator paradigm and to realize the potentials that lie in this discovery, Eisler uses the conceptual framework of systems theory.

> Within the perspective of this new conceptual framework, as incorporated in Cultural Transformation theory, what we have been examining are two aspects of social dynamics. The first relates to social stability - how for thousands of years there were human societies that were organized in a way that is different from the way we have been taught all human systems are organized. The second relates to how social systems, like other systems, can, and do, undergo fundamental change. (Eisler 1988: 60)

By quoting some of the Old Testament's exemplary stories about the inhumane treatment of women and "infidels", up to the legitimization of brutal rape with a divine moral (Eisler 1988 98ff), Eisler shows how deep the transformation changed people's mindset and world view up to today, resulting in a "systems-induced blindness" (Eisler 1988: 99).

> So effectively has the imposition of a dominator morality been that even today men and women who think of themselves as good, moral people are able to read passages like this without questioning how a just and righteous God could order such horrible and inhuman acts. (Eisler 1988: 98)

The analysis of the thorough transformation of the social system from partnership to dominance is crucial to develop strategies that could support and enhance the system break which is, according to many system thinkers, currently happening in our social system as our (social and cultural) evolution reached another bifurcation point.

The crucial point in the transformation is, obviously, to be found in the spiritual/religious realm. The transformation process could only be successful if people's spirituality, their complete belief system with the Great Mother Goddess and her connectedness with nature and the female, fertility and harmony, with its energetic peace concept where peace was based on communication, cooperation and harmony, would be totally turned around and replaced with an autocratic, male warrior god and his resort to the one truth that from now on would regulate good and bad, right and wrong. The methodical devaluation of women to an economic trade object in the possession of men that was a necessary component of this turnaround was only possible if the old belief system had been totally eradicated from people's minds.

> Clearly the morality enforcing women's sexual slavery to men was imposed to meet the economic requirements of a rigidly male-dominant system that property was transmitted from father to son and that the benefits from women's and children's labor accrue to male. It was also imposed to meet the political and ideological requirement that the social realities of the old order, in which women were sexually, economically, and politically free agents, and in which the Goddess was the supreme deity, be fundamentally reversed. For only through such a reversal could a power structure based on rigid rankings be maintained. (Eisler 1988: 100)

Eisler indicates that we are talking about a process that took millennia to be completed, and she explains that in the case of the Canaanite people, it was guided by leading priest castes that were busy re-writing the religious texts and myths, which led to the texts that are part of the Old Testament of our current Bible. As we can read there, war, fights, and violence were considered accepted means to realize the transformation; the "13 Hebrew tribes" the Bible talks about are the former nomadic conquerors whose atrocities are sanctified by their "divine mission" as being led in all their actions by the one and only god - this paradigm shift was reached through what Eisler calls "skillful re-mything" (Eisler 1988: 102).

I.5.1.3 The hierarchic holdback

According to Veronika Kauffmann, hierarchy is to be understood as the underlying concept of the patriarchal world order. By identifying hierarchy as nothing more than a "thought construct" that has been in place all through recorded history and therefore is seen as "natural", she contributes to Eisler's project of making visible that what we see as "natural" and "normal" in human relationships is not the only possible way of perceiving reality. Quite the opposite, hierarchy is really only one of different possible ordering principles of society:

> However, hierarchy is a map, it is not the territory. It is a thought construct superimposed upon life as a classifying and ordering schematic. It is a norm employed as a tool to control for uncertainty and irregularity and so to preserve the status quo. In my view, we find ourselves lost in the thicket of dynamic complexity because we adhere to such an outlived linear and dualistic cosmology. (Kauffmann 1997)

Furthermore, we could conclude, that hierarchy is a totally simplifying principle, since it is based on a linear and dualistic world view. Seeing the world through the lenses of hierarchy narrows the perspective down to dichotomies: good or bad, useful or useless, self or other. "Hierarchy presupposes antithesis as a matter of definition. Individuals and societies locked in the hierarchic model require an*other* as an *object,* a foil, to profile themselves and, so it is believed, to develop their potential. We call it 'survival of the fittest'" (Kauffmann 1997). In this point of view, the competitor society developed out of the concept of hierarchy, or out of the dominator model of society organization. Since hierarchy doesn't work without a bottom, it is impossible to achieve real democratic equality as long as hierarchy is the principle that structures our thoughts in a mostly unconscious way. The only way to overcome hierarchic limits is, therefore, the individual struggle and to look for ourselves only. This attitude is, of course, totally incompatible with the egalitarian principle of a partnership society.

Kauffmann believes, too, that humanity is at the brink of a bifurcation point, and that the main question, if we are running into breakdown or if we will manage to reach breakthrough, will depend on the creation of awareness in the social system for an understanding of social reality that hierarchy is not a natural nor a necessary way to structure our world.

> Such an attitudinal shift can happen when we recognize that the hierarchic model is no longer adequate: in a world of dynamic complexity, the static model constrains us in an atavistic framework. In an environment in flux, ever-changing conditions demand an adaptive model for sustainability. In becoming aware of the structural coercion in the hierarchic model, we can attend to our manner of relating, from contenders to partners, from boxing to dancing. (Kauffmann 1997)

Applying a systemic point of view, we could say that only through a change in the collective consciousness of humankind, breakthrough will be possible.

I.5.2 A History of Peace?

While in *The Chalice and the Blade,* Eisler is mainly focusing on proving that partnership-cultures have really exited as egalitarian farming societies in a much more frequent and successful mode in humanity's prehistory and that in prehistory, this was actually the more widespread form of organization in societies, specifically culturally rich societies, Elise Boulding also contributes some examples of cultures that did transform over time from a dominator to a partnership model of a society. In her book *Cultures of Peace. The Hidden Side of History* (2000), Boulding brings two concrete examples of societies that completely changed from a warrior-paradigm to a peace-paradigm. Her first example, the impressive story of the Indian Emperor Ashoka, also tells us that single visionaries, meaning individuals in power, who took the chance to change a common paradigm by using this power of theirs, have and will always play a significant role in the realization of cultural transformation. Ashoka, Boulding rephrases, "who, after great conquests of nearby peoples in the third century B.C.E., repented of his war making and issued the Rock Edicts, calling on all neighboring kingdoms as well as his own people to live in peace and joy with one another" (Boulding E. 2000: 24). Boulding's second example is not less striking as it is about a story we all know and studied in history classes, but maybe with a different focus: it's the story of the Vikings, who were considered at their times as the "scourge of Europe", a prototype of a warring, heroic people, whose pride was made up by conquest and pillaging. As if almost suddenly, these people changed their strategies from conquest to trade and negotiation, which went along with a change in their way of living towards settlement and farming. Today, as Boulding rightly states, Scandinavia is regarded as the most peaceful (internally; this is not saying anything about the region's connections to war and conflict in other regions; neither does it say anything about the qualitative meaning of the word *peaceful* in this regard) and also the most prosperous and egalitarian/partnership-oriented region in Europe.

This example suggests that Eisler's important account of the transformation of partnership societies into dominator societies in prehistoric times, has also happened in the reverse order in known history as in the case of the Scandinavians/Vikings. The transformation must therefore be seen as possible in both directions.

Boulding's important contribution to Eisler's theory is her focus on the world's current social system. While Eisler proves in detail how the partnership-model was the common model of societal organization in prehistoric times, Boulding is adding recent and present historical examples of such an orientation in societies. To emphasize this, she uses utopian visions of egalitarian, peaceful societies of our times. In a chapter called *The Passion for Utopia* (Boulding E. 2000: 29 ff), she makes clear that the very ability to imagine a better, just world and the belief in its possibility is the most necessary prerequisite for social change. In this way, utopian imaginaries in their different forms, as novels, poems, songs, or even paintings can contribute a lot to an increasing awareness and to a concretion of what should become our reality. "Under the pressure of social upheaval, the archetypal vision is transformed into concrete imagery that answers specific social needs and dissatisfactions" (Boulding E. 2000: 30). Concluding that utopia always is the other, the opposite even of reality, Boulding observes that the attempt to realize utopian ideas always implies a revolutionary transformation of society, which most of the time includes the use of violence even though the goal of the revolution might be peace, equality, and justice. "During the crisis, when the time is ripe, anything goes. There is time enough later for the gentler human virtues to reassert themselves. This argument operates as strongly for religious as for secular revolutionary change" (Boulding E. 2000: 36). A complete reorganization of society will most likely not be possible without having to deal with resistance against it, having to fight the established forces in a society who don't want to give up their comfortable and powerful positions.

This of course was also the case in Nicaragua, but there is evidence that right after the victory of the revolution what Boulding calls the "gentler virtues" came to rule, which meant for example that many of the soldiers of the dictator's National Guard were surprised with mercy and even amnesty (if they couldn't be identified as war criminals) rather than death or torture. (Der Spiegel 20/08/1979: 96). One of the first official actions of the new leadership was the complete abolishment of death penalty and the reduction of the maximum penalty to 30 years of prison on the 21st of August, 1979 (Dietrich 1988: 326) - only one month after their takeover.

Although the Sandinistas finally couldn't go through with this first attempt to at once finish with any inhuman treatment, even for those people who were responsible for atrocities, cruelties, and terror during the dictatorship, the few records of human rights violations in the aftermath of the so-called "Red Christmas" in 1981, has to be seen in the light of the Contra War, according to Dietrich. He furthermore emphasizes that the lapses in this respect, although lamentable, didn't get out of control. He especially mentions the treatment of opposition leaders (imprisonment, censorship etc.) and isolated cases of mistreatment or even killings of Contra fighters or affiliates outside of the war zones. Dietrich argues, that first of all, the country had declared the state of exception until the US would stop intervening and sending money, weapons, and fighters into their country. The limitation of democratic freedoms like the freedom of press or assembly is common in a state of exception for self-defense. However, human rights organizations like Amnesty International note positively how the Sandinista leadership, except in very few cases, routinely brought their own functionaries to justice for any illegal inhumane actions they committed or commanded.

But aside of this, Elise Boulding's observation seems also to be true for Nicaragua: that the political strategies used to achieve the utopia they long for often destroy the idealistic and noble goals (Boulding 2000: 30). She also states that although there is no evidence that the resort to violence predetermines the failure of a utopian movement, since nonviolent utopias also fail, it is clear that "[...] generalized violence endangers the utopian commitment" (Boulding 2000: 37).

I.5.3 Partnership

How does a partnership model of society then look like, in practice, and how do we get there? Speaking with Ervin Laszlo, Riane Eisler argues that we can transform our society if we consciously decide to do so, since "[...] bifurcations in human social systems also involve a large element of choice" (Eisler 1988: 186). As I already mentioned, Eisler strives to prove that a partnership organization of society is a realistic possibility. She therefore rejects envisioning that kind of society as utopian. And since the arguments for the cultural transformation towards a partnership society are pragmatic in the sense that without this shift, there will probably be no other alternative in the long run than breakdown or extinction of humanity and most life on earth, she calls her visionary partnership world a pragmatopia.

> It won't be a perfect place. But it will no longer be a world of top-down rankings of domination - man over woman, person over person, nation over nation, and humankind over nature. It will be a place where beliefs and social structures support relations based on partnership - on mutual respect, mutual benefit, mutual caring. It will be a far less violent, much more humane and equitable place. (Eisler 2004)

In a systemic perspective, partnership is a specific form of relation. "The partnering concept engages individual entities in dynamic bond to create a complex system, a composite whole greater than the sum of its parts" (Kauffmann 1997). In a partnership society, power is based on responsibility and caring, rather than hierarchy and competition. In a partnership society, we see a new kind of science emerge, a science that takes a holistic perspective and focuses on relationships rather than hierarchies (Eisler 1988: 190). In a partnership society, dialog and cooperation are the basic attitudes, aiming at retaining individual "uniqueness" and reaching to a "common ground". In a partnership society, "partners [are] honoring essential difference in one another" (Kauffmann 1997). The important aspect is the basic understanding that by relating to the other, both can only gain and grow together since their different capacities of the partners expand the capacities of the partnership as a whole.

We can see this approach in connection to the insight that human evolution marks a revolutionary shift from biological to cultural evolution that happens through mutual learning, rather than through genetic mutation (formulated in Chapter I.4.3). "In the dialogue among the multiple aspects of separate and mutual awareness, second order knowing happens. Neither partner dominates; none possess privileged access to transcendental Truth. Together, they emerge a highly charged self-referential system" (Kauffmann 1997). In tune with Eisler, Kauffmann understands the human desire for partnership and unity as being suppressed over millennia but she too thinks that it's a human characteristic too strong to be destroyed. She sees the alliance of two partners in marriage as a proof for this longing; and indeed, we're talking of a bond blessed through a spiritual ceremony and the symbolic exchange of rings; a ritualistic procedure that seems outdated in our times, and even proven wrong by the number of divorces; but still, our "romantic mind" seems to make us blind for these facts or, the desire for alliance and community is the stronger attractor.

The importance of the smallest partnership system in a society, the nuclear family, is going to be a matter of practical analysis in the case study on Nicaragua. Although the basic idea of founding a family corresponds with the human desire for partnership, we can conclude that the leading dominator paradigm had also a severe influence in the constitution of the family. The existing hierarchies and fixed structures in the family have become expressions of the dominator structure itself; not to be generalist, let's say in some cases. Maybe the smallest units of a system have to be the most stable ones to keep the whole system stable. That would mean that a paradigm shift in these smallest units is crucial for any system change totake place. But maybe, the smallest structures also need most time and awareness to be changed... since they seem to represent the most natural of human relationships. As we will see, Nicaraguan women tend to have a lot to say about their role and relationship at home.

II. NICARAGUA - A CASE STUDY ON REVOLUTION

Household Earth and Principle Hope

In the introduction for her part of the book *The Future. Images and Processes* (1995) where Elise Boulding published a collection of essays of both herself and her deceased husband Kenneth, she writes what in her opinion differentiates his work from hers. One important difference is her view of the world as a system: while Kenneth coined the metaphor of the *spaceship earth,* she likes to see the earth rather as a household where everybody has his/her place. And she states further:

> The day-to-day actions that shape the future have an unending fascination for me. The underside of the social systems, where private behaviors gradually, over time, pattern public usage, reveals the marginal persons and the marginal roles that are often missed in general systems analysis. The change points in society are found on city streets, on school playgrounds, in the privacy of the home, and in all types of little-recognized civic spaces, from neighborhoods to global organizations operating through communication networks unique to this century. Over and over again, the interpersonal and the local intersect with the macrosystem to produce new futures. (Boulding E. 1995: 90)

At the starting point of the second part of this book, I would like to say with Elise Boulding that the analysis of these "small bits and pieces" of human society and the focus on the individual are maybe the expression of an alternative approach in system theory; an approach that might as well be called a feminine or feminist approach, although she herself doesn't call it like that. It includes also a strong re-emphasis on the feminist motto that the personal is political. The following case-study is about personal stories, ideas, emotions, and relations.

Having said this I hope that I made clear what this study is not about, too: it is not about the big decisions and influences in the macrosystem that led to the success and then slow breakdown of the revolutionary movement in Nicaragua. I want to go with E. Boulding and say that it's the small stories that interest me. The "daily choices" that, in her and my opinion, are a main motor of change in a system. To be aware of the interdependence between the personal and the political, the private and the public in a society is crucial for a successful systems change.

> The partnership model has a different core configuration: a **democratic and egalitarian structure in both the family and the state or tribe;** equal partnership between women and men; and a low degree of built-in violence because force is not needed to maintain rigid rankings of domination. (Eisler 2004)

Before starting, I would like to make a remark about the Nicaraguan revolution as such. I think I made it clear enough why I chose Nicaragua as my case study, but apart from my personal experiences there is another reason: although I'm going to interpret the revolution as finally failed in the sense that the cultural transformation from a dominator to a partnership society didn't completely work out, I do believe that it may be the best example of a national movement aiming at realizing a totally different society based on equality, mutual learning, and cooperation in recent history. The Nicaraguan revolution didn't lead to the realization of the utopian society it aimed at, but without seeing that as a final judgment, it's possible to add the little word "yet" in the end and the perspective changes from a frustrated, pessimistic one to an optimistic, active one.

> [...] if we look at modern progressive movements not as failures, but as incomplete processes, there is realistic hope for the future. We can then explore what our next steps should be and get on with the most important human enterprise: constructing social systems that support rather than inhibit and distort our enormous human capacities for consciousness, caring, and creativity. (Eisler 2004)

The question that I'm interested to answer with this case study is, if it is true, that this partnership-oriented model, based on the principle that a system only functions in the long term when all its parts are included, involved and respected, was, to a certain extent at least, put in place in Nicaragua in the framework of the revolution, and if this can be seen as one of the major reasons for its primary success. The question connected to this is, if the nearly all-encompassing movement that brought forward the revolution can be analyzed as an example of the mechanisms at work according to systems theories. The energy that has been released in the case of the revolution was an unimaginably strong driving force. If the amount of energy in a system never changes, but just shifts within the system, then to do some research on the high concentration of energy in this case, why it happened and how it materialized, could be important for the field of peace and conflict studies. This is also promising if we understand energy as something "neutral", that can be used for any kind of purpose, good or bad. The role of *archetypal imaginations,* following Jung, Sheldrake et al., will be analyzed using original testimonials (interviews and autobiographies) and cultural manifestations like poetry, utopian novels, etc., to find out the motifs that made this joint venture so strong in the beginning.

Finally, it seems crucial to find out what made the energy decline or, systemically speaking, shift back into different, maybe unconscious, fields. Did it go side by side with the going back from a partnership-oriented model to a hierarchical, power-oriented, self-centered and formalistic society?

II.2 The Nicaraguán Revolution as a Dionysian Ritual

> During the ten years of Sandinista government, the most beautiful thing for me - and it's what I feel as my greatest loss since our defeat - is having participated in a great collective project. It offered extraordinary hope, and it created a tremendous communal energy. It was like living inside a mighty river that constantly renewed you - spiritually, even physically. (Belli in Randall 1994: 185)

In the first years after the victory of the revolution in 1979, the atmosphere in Nicaragua was described by so many who participated as a state of collective energy, ecstasy, and the overwhelming feeling that dreams can be made true, that the power of the people can change the world. The following part of a poem by Daisy Zamora makes a good example for this enthusiastic, optimist spirit that characterized these Dionysian years.

[...]

Everything we said came true and the words are
alive, they live and now we can catch them as one
holds a guis, *a needle duck, a little woodcock, not*
to do them harm but let them soar returning to that
loveliest summer at La Azucena.

Our words have acquired the concrete shape of things,
and schools, crafts workshops, agricultural production
and cattle development centers have found their way to
your San Juan River.
Those words have become libraries,
clinics, cooperatives, and in the old port of San Carlos there
is the first Culture House that anyone can remember.
[...]

(From "Letter to Coronel Urtecho", Zamora 1993: 128f.)

Reading through the testimonials of Nicaraguan women after the electoral defeat of the Sandinista government in 1990 shows how "Sandino's daughters", e.g. the women who were most actively involved in the revolution and later on as politicians, built up their identity as women and gained a feminist consciousness over time, connected with a high level of empowerment for this type of woman who grew up within a very patriarchal central American (macho) society. These women, it seems, lived through the seesaw process of self- and society transformation, or in other words, they practically lived a holistic model of social change that was reflected in their personal lives as well as through the work they were doing as revolutionaries.

Reading about their male counterparts, it seems that this holistic approach was missing: the women are blaming the men for either deliberately or unconsciously still being bound to the "old", traditional concept of power and hierarchy. If this assessment is true, the crucial question would be, why had the men such a hard time (in comparison to the women) in putting their common vision of an equal and just society that has been developed by women and men alike into practice, in bringing it down from the ideological to the practical level of action and reaction.

II.2.1 Myths and Archetypes

My hypothesis is that the very nature of the revolutionary Nicaragua as a utopian vision of the future is, indeed, a reflection of a society based on cooperation and partnership rather than domination, once again following Riane Eisler's terminology. So, we could argue, in a culture where partnership, cooperation, and caring are terms associated with femininity, and where girls grow up with these values, it must be easier for women to wholeheartedly embrace this new vision and commit themselves fully to realize it on all levels of their lives. On the other hand, we are talking about a society where "macho" values are the praise-worthy attributes of men, which makes it harder for them to support the elevation of "softer" values, especially when it comes down to their own lives and would affect their own manhood and macho identity.

Finally, we could ask, how was it at all possible that the revolution could be realized on the grounds of the values of partnership, if these are values that men don't appraise naturally. The answer lies, I believe, somewhere in the Jungian collective unconscious and the archetype theory: the archetypes of the hero and liberator are very strong archetypes in human history. The hero has been identified as usually male throughout the last thousands of years, according to Eisler (1988). So, the true revolutionary is representing the prototype of a liberator-hero, who in the case of Nicaragua was a simple young man with a uniform, a poem on his lips and a musical instrument in one, a rifle in the other hand. Within this archetype, the erotic component is an important one and the attractiveness of these young heroes was increasing with the increasing energy level in the society when more and more people joined forces in favor of the FSLN's goals and their vision of the new Nicaragua, and when the heroic figures started to lose their lives for the higher goal, which elevated them to a martyr and super-hero status. With Che Guevara's slogan that "the true revolutionary is guided by feelings of love" (in Boulding E. 1995: 89), the womanizer-image was depicted and we can be sure that they did their best to live up to it - while side by side a sexual liberation took place that empowered women in the guerrilla as it fueled the Dionysian component of energy, love, ecstasy, and altered states of consciousness in an extreme situation where life could end at any time.

Vidaluz Meneses, a prominent revolutionary and poet, who later on became active as a feminist recently published a book called La lucha es el más alto de los cantos (2006. Translation: The struggle is the highest of songs) about her time in the *Leonel Rugama Brigade*, a group of 31 artists. In 1983, this brigade spent 17 days with the Sandinista troops fighting against a Contra offensive with the aim to "entreniendo y culturizando a los heroicos combatientes herederos de Sandino" (Chinchilla 2007, translation: train and culturize the heroic combatants and heirs of Sandino), in the words of *El Nuevo Diario,* the leftist one of the two big newspapers in Nicaragua. Meneses herself describes their task a bit different: the Brigade was supposed to bring joy and encouragement to the soldiers. But *El Nuevo Diario* goes even further and celebrates the book as a reflection of the poetic nature of the Nicaraguan people. "En casi todos los frentes de guerra que visitó la Brigada en el período referido, se encontró con poetas, músicos y cantores populares" (Chinchilla 2007, translation: On almost all the battle fronts that the Brigade visited in the referred period, they met poets, musicians, and popular singers.).

But the really interesting part of this article is the example for this "poetic nature" that *El Nuevo Diario,* quoting from Meneses' book, is using as a "paradigmatic case" of a 30-year-old soldier who sang a song that he himself had composed:

"Yo quiero ser miliciano / para defender mi patria / combatir a los traidores / y que me quieran / las muchachas" (Chinchilla 2007, translation: I want to be a militiaman / to defend my fatherland / to fight the traitors / and that I would be loved / by the girls).

Not only can the poetic quality of this short song text be questioned, especially stylized to a proof for the poetic nature of the Nicaraguans as a people, but it is, following the analysis above, rather a proof for the presence of the hero and liberator archetype (the tough good-looking revolutionary with the guitar in his hands, as described above), a very "manly" stereotype, whose persistence was maybe one of the stumbling blocks in the transformation process towards partnership. It is really significant, that this archetype-stereotype still seems to be persistent (at least in the heads of some male journalist) in the year 2007.

The persistence of the hero-archetype led to fatal consequences after the Sandinista National Liberation Front won the war against the dictatorship in July, 1979. Gioconda Belli tells about the seductive appeal of this myth reflecting on her personal low when she gave up on her own abilities, goals and visions, given the unique chance to revolutionize the Nicaraguan national TV according to her own creative ideas, to please a man who exuded a heroic presence she couldn't resist. But apart from this gender imbalance that was recreated over and over again through the myth of the male hero and the female admirer, who then becomes the good and caring partner and mother, Belli tells of serious political consequences of the aura of invulnerability and indestructibility the revolutionary heroes carried in the first months and years after the success. They were not only survivors while so many of their fellow combatants lost their lives, but they were also the ones who distributed the power among them and thus they became carriers of this power. In this situation they underestimated the possibilities of US intervention, believes Belli:

> (I)mmer wieder gewann ich die beunruhigende Erkenntnis, dass jene Männer an dem verführerischen Bild klebengeblieben waren, das sie sich von sich selbst geschaffen hatten: das Bild, das ihnen die Augen der Menge am Tag des Sieges zurückspiegelte. Sie fühlten sich ungemein schlau und geschickt, wie eine Mischung politischer Frechdachse und heroischer, sehr männlicher Kreuzritter. In dieser Haltung stellten sie sich gefährlichen Herausforderungen, die eine ruhigere Betrachtung verdient hätten, eine Reife, die das überwältigende Gefühl, an der Macht zu sein,

> sie nicht mehr gewinnen ließ. (Belli 2002: 362. Translation: Time and again I came to the alarming perception that these men were still sticking to the seductive image they created of themselves: the image they saw reflected in the eyes of the crowd on the day of victory. They felt extremely clever and smart, like a mixture of political rascals and heroic, very masculine crusaders. In this mindset they faced dangerous challenges, which would have needed a more careful consideration, a maturity they couldn't reach within this overwhelming feeling of being in power.)

It is this irrational feeling, a kind of ecstasy that is in part responsible for the failure to create the balanced society after the phase of chaotic, collective, Dionysian energy. As if the strength, almost invincibility of the collective had turned into a sense of invincibility of the individuals, who felt most responsible for the victory. The powerful hero archetype, supported by so many, particularly women like Belli herself who couldn't understand herself anymore after several years, can be seen as one of many conditions that made this fatal overestimation of a few possible.

II.2.1.1 The Fallen Hero (A fairy tale)

	(Translation:
Los que te hicimos hombre, Edén	We who made you a man, Edén
te deshombramos	we took away your manhood
solo eres dueno ahora	Now you're no more than the master
de un cero en la historia.	of a cero in history.)

(Belli in Bardini: 2003)

Love is the underlying motto and motivation of the Nicaraguan revolution. And as the simple song text of the guerillero above seems to tell us, love, or rather, being loved, was one of the core motivations for many of the fighters. To feel loved and respected are the core motivators for every human action, according to recent neurobiological findings, as we saw in Chapter I.4.3.

In a society marked by a culture of "machismo", the opinion that "one woman is not enough for a real man" is often to be heard (Lancaster 1992). As Lancaster shows, many Nicaraguan men want to love and be loved by as many women as possible. This behavior is often accompanied by veritable "proof", or "trophy" of this manifold love-ability, which is fathering numerous children with several women - this account is earning a man respect by other men.

The revolution with its power to create heroes (and martyrs) can thus be seen as an additional method to gain respect (primarily by men) and love (primarily by women).

Within this archetypal depiction of the revolutionary hero we find the story of Edén Pastora. It is a unique, incomprehensible story and therefore worth telling. On the 22nd of August of 1978, Edén Pastora was leading a group of 25 Sandinista fighters to storm and occupy the Nicaraguan National Palace. The occupation lasted 45 hours and ended with a total success of the Sandinistas: the liberation of 59 party members held as political prisoners, the public reading of Sandinista pamphlets on the radio, 500.000 US Dollars in cash, an airplane for the 25 guerrilleros/as, and free passage.

This was the most successful operation in the history of the FSLN, and it paved the path for the final success of the revolution. Of course, this operation was also very important for the degree of popularity and credibility of the FSLN in the population. As it was a very risky operation, all the fighters had to use numbers instead of their usual war-names and so Pastora became known as Comandante Cero. For Pastora, who was frequently criticized for his risk-taking behavior out of his craving for recognition, this name didn't seem to fit. And so he couldn't resist showing his uncovered face when he boarded the plane in the pose of the winner - a behavior that left his desire for respect, love, and recognition uncovered, and that showed once again that he didn't fear death but would do anything to become a hero - or a martyr. But the photo of Pastora in his winner-pose traveled around the world. No doubt that his fearlessness made him a great fighter, and in the struggles that led to the ultimate success on July 19th, 1979, the Somoza forces thought Pastora to be the most dangerous of all Sandinista Commanders. He had become a war hero, was celebrated and - in his own imagery - loved. He went as far as to refer to himself as "el comandante más querido" (Bardini 2003).

After the revolutionary success though, Pastora was struggling with the feeling of being ignored. He didn't get a seat in the front row of the party, did not become one of the nine members of the National Directorate, nor did he get a leading position in the government. As vice minister for the interior, he soon enough felt frustrated and disillusioned about the revolution. He blamed Daniel Ortega for his ideological closeness to communism and the party leaders for taking over the pompous residences of Somoza and his friends instead of helping the poor population and left the political floor. *Comandante Cero* had no say in this arena, so he went back to what he knew best: fighting. Consequently, he founded a small army from his base in Costa Rica and announced that he would fight the FSLN. Since the CIA was already funding the counterrevolutionary forces based in the north (around the Honduran border), they now took the chance to fund Pastora's group as well, which was attacking from the south.

In his private life, Pastora pays in to the "macho" tradition and fathered 19 children from 4 wives. But even here, the guerrillero who wanted to be loved seems to have failed. Three of his marriages broke apart, owed to his life as a revolutionary, as he is said to complain.

Pastora's story is tragic indeed: he couldn't sustain his hero image, and no attempt to kill him succeeded so that he could have become a martyr. In 1984, he survived an assassination attempt when he was giving a press talk in a town called Pencas close to the border to Costa Rica. Although 11 people died, he and his wife got injured but survived miraculously.

Being denied the honor of a hero or a martyr, Edén Pastora keeps trying to re-gain the love of the Nicaraguan people and makes himself look silly. In 2001, he run for elections of the mayor of Managua, the Nicaraguan capital, and in 2006, he even run for president against his arch rival Daniel Ortega. He received 0.29% of the votes - not far from zero.

Thinking about Pastora's story and reading about different interpretations of the story of the "fallen angel", or Lucifer/Satan, some interesting thoughts come to mind. In the discussion about the first fallen angel, who he was and where the story comes from, I frequently found one interpretation that has to do with either Lucifer and/or Satan, who are believed to have been archangels very high up in the heavenly hierarchy who, having received a free will, finally stood up against God's autocratic regime in heaven, which resulted in a "war in heaven", with the consequence that they lost this war and were thrown out of heaven, together with a number of angels as their followers, from where they fell on earth - the fallen angels. The first sin of Lucifer was, according to different theological teachers, the sin of pride, which made him aspire for a position or a kind of likeness to God that was against the creator's will. But since the whole fallen angel story is a complicated issue for clericals, they are also not sure about the angel's sin. Pride is one frequent assumption, another one comes from the 13th century theologian Scotus: "Scotus, however [...], teaches that this sin was not pride properly so called, but should rather be described as a species of spiritual lust" (Kent 1908).

There seem to be a lot of similarities between the fallen angel story and the story of our fallen hero, Edén Pastora. And although Pastora clearly acted mainly out of hurt pride as an egocentric individual who always strove to be the center of public attention, the question has to be asked if such a rebellion against the movement he had contributed so much to would be even possible if there weren't autocratic tendencies in the Sandinista leadership of the early years after the revolution. Or in other words: if the Sandinistas had lived up to their ideals, first and foremost the ideal of equality, right from the beginning; if there weren't a hierarchic order of things, then how could a hero fall down to the bottom at all?

As for this book, Edén Pastora is a Dionysian figure who, by consciously taking the risk of sacrificing himself stood up against the Apollonian order that he saw being established without being listened to; he did so by acting irrationally, desperately trying to bring the ecstatic atmosphere back when gripped by the collective spirit of the masses, he was their hero. He hazards the consequences of annihilation for the myth to resurge.

With this I don't want to say that there was no serious attempt to create the new society. But the hero archetype was, in my opinion, one obstacle to this enterprise that shouldn't be underestimated. When we think about a hero, we imagine a young, strong, fearless and brave male person - that's how we have been socialized. The creation of such heroes is necessary to win a war. In the Nicaraguan revolution, there was a unique chance to create a new image of the hero, an image that could be male or female, and I believe that to a certain degree, this happened. But the female hero was not depicted very often without a specific connotation; a connotation that was more and more emphasized during the war: the female feature of motherhood; the archetype of the loving mother.

II.2.1.2 Motherhood

> As we have seen, mothers in Nicaragua promoted and even fought in the revolution and war. Nonetheless, my interviews with the Mothers also revealed a narrative that privileged mothers' labor

> (both birthing labor and the labor of raising a child) as an exclusive source of knowledge concerning the costs of war. (Bayard de Volo 2001: 64)

What can be read in this quote is that women through their connection to motherhood, although they are as capable of armed struggle as men (a capacity they proved as guerrilla fighters) are more prone to act towards stopping the bloodshed than men. This is of course a provocative assumption, but in her interviews with Nicaraguan mothers, Lorraine Bayard de Volo was confronted with exactly this idea expressed in different forms from woman to woman. Quote Dona Lourdes: "The one who feels [the loss of a child] is the mother. It is a feeling that is never erased. Every minute we remember because we mothers are the ones that gave the child its food, loved it" (Bayard de Volo 2001: 65).

Interviewed mothers relate the above mentioned "mother-specific labor" only partly to the experience of pregnancy and the birth itself, but they also speak, like Dona Lourdes, about the labor of nursing, cleaning, feeding the child after giving birth. It is common in a patriarchal society that these tasks are almost exclusively assigned to the mother.

However, it could be argued that a real transformation of society towards partnership, nonviolence, and an energetic understanding of human relations can only be realized completely if these stereotypical gender distinctions are to be overcome. The essentialist argument that women are naturally different from men through their experience of giving birth, breastfeeding their babies etc. can, in my opinion, not be proven right or wrong until there has been no serious attempt of a critical mass of men in a society to share all the tasks related to raising children, except those that are only doable by women due to their biological nature.

I want to argue furthermore, that a father, who would from the first day of the baby's life on take the same share of responsibility for its well-being as a mother, could develop an emotional connectedness with his child that's as close as the mother's. I also do believe that this transformation in the minds (that has to be a joint-venture of women and men, since it's in many cases also the women who don't want to give up their dominant position at home) that would be reflected in a family organized as a real partnership, where both partners share their power as responsibility. As we will see in Chapter II.2.4, in a university, one single woman (Vidaluz Meneses) was able to transform the institutionalized structure considerably from a hierarchical towards a partnership way. In Nicaragua, it became socially acceptable through the revolution that women are in the same positions as men outside their houses, that they take over public positions, and that they can succeed even as high-ranking military officers. However, the traditional gender roles in the houses seem to have been widely untouched by these developments.

> In sum, because fathers had not physically experienced pregnancy and the birth of their children, and, if present at all, were less involved in the daily domestic life and had less contact with their children, most of the mothers interviewed said that fathers felt the death of a child less intensely. The daily routine was less disrupted for the father and his emotional ties to his children were weaker, so the sudden severing of those ties was less dramatic. (Bayard de Volo 2001: 67)

The identity of a man in the new Nicaragua had indeed little to do with his responsibilities and activities as a father and husband. And although this lack slowly started to be perceived as a real threat to the revolutionary project, the FSLN with its mass organizations failed to create a real remedy for this identity crisis. With the powerful hero image in place, the loving father who stays home with his family was not an ideal to be followed for many. The culture of machismo, which was traditionally a very strong part of Nicaraguan collective identity, is totally opposed to any kind of equal society; and it clearly had its troubles with the gender equality Sandinista leaders were trying to prove possible.

> Clearly, in many homes, there was estrangement and even animosity between fathers and their children. Thus, while mothers were put on a pedestal, fathers rarely measured up to the fuzzily developed paternal ideal. Within the system of machismo, which prioritizes sexual conquest and virility over paternal responsibility and affection, there was little status to be attained through this paternal ideal and not much of a basis upon which to build a collective identity based on fatherhood. (Bayard de Volo 2001: 69)

In Bayard de Volo's analysis, the Sandinista's glorification of motherhood had a lot to do with the failure of real emancipation of women. The essentialist argument that mothers are more prone to peace, care, and sacrificing themselves than men first led women to play a crucial role in the realization of the country's far-reaching campaigns for the education and betterment of the masses (literacy crusade, health crusade etc.), but soon enough it reinforced the old gender divisions. Soon enough, the essentialist argument was used to keep women in their traditional places and led to the exclusion of women from the draft for 17- to 25- year-old men put in place in 1983.

The persistence of machismo in society, it seems, got in the way of a different reality; a scenario that has been there as a vision and named the "new man" and "new woman" in the "new Nicaragua". But the creation of the mother-archetype and the persistence of the hero-archetype strongly opposed the development of a real partnership society. As we will see in Chapter II.2.2, this inflexible structuring of genders created problems especially for the intellectual women who were from the beginning involved in the new government structures.

> On the one hand, women whose subjectivities went beyond the traditional feminine lifestyles, particularly those who leaned toward feminist interpretations of society, found their options restricted. On the other hand, many women who still perceived themselves to be on the losing end of the revolution - either economically or through the loss of loved ones - despite Sandinista propaganda attempts to draw them in, turned a sympathetic ear to anti-Sandinista discourse. (Bayard de Volo 2001: 102)

With the glorification of stereotypically feminine attributes in the mother image, the revolution must have lost its credibility for a big number of women who took up "male" roles during the revolutionary period and therefore made a big step towards partnership. The after-revolutionary idealization of motherhood is one of the reasons we can name as in part responsible for the getting-out-of-balance and later for the collapse of the new society the Sandinistas wanted to create. It is important to see that it's not only the attribution of "motherly" traits (emotional, caring, collectively thinking, sacrificing her own well-being for others etc. - altogether traits that have a lot to do with the energetic, relational principle of Dionysus) to women that caused the problem, but also and most importantly the resulting non-takeover of men of these attributes - since they were almost exclusively connected with motherhood and motherhood was excluding men. This failure of men in their houses and men in leadership roles to take over some of these "motherly" values led to the hierarchical Apollonian structures we see in place again, soon after the revolutionary success.

> Crossing gender boundaries during exceptional circumstances, such as popular insurrection, did not secure women an equal

> position in the 'New Society', nor did it fundamentally alter traditional notions of femininity. During the post-triumph euphoria, visions of fundamental social change, including equal rights for women, competed with a popular yearning to return to normalcy, especially within the home. With the enemy defeated, the 'guerrilla girls' could lay down their weapons, return home, and bear and raise children in a new, revolutionary society. (Bayard de Volo 2001: 38)

What Bayard de Volo calls "normalcy" is of course the natural enemy of society transformation, and so it gets clearer and clearer how deeply rooted the traditional organization of society has been in Nicaragua. The dream of the new world did in most cases not include a serious reflection on and revision of the traditional setup of interpersonal relations. Even though qualities stamped as female tended to be more respected in the new Nicaragua than before, they still were seen as inherent feminine qualities; and although qualities stamped as male tended to be criticized by feminist tendencies more openly than ever before, they still were seen as inherent masculine qualities. There was certain openness for change, but it got stuck on the superficial. Finally, the patriarchal composition of the society could not be transformed, according to Bayard de Volo: "However, as in typical male-dominated societies, the most respected traits, those that conferred status and power, were those associated with men, and the glorification of stereotypical feminine traits actually worked to keep women in their separate and unequal places" (Bayard de Volo 2001: 102).

On the other hand, the ideal of motherhood was also intimately connected to the revolution itself, and this should not be overlooked in this analysis. The connection between the revolution and the Dionysian and with the female as such is very important. The collective people's movement that led to the fall of the dictatorship is for many Nicaraguans directly connected with emotions, love, and tenderness - virtues that are closely related with motherhood. Gioconda Belli thus tells of the revolution as giving birth collectively. Her description is full of Dionysian elements and shows impressively how the female principle, fertility, giving birth, energy, ecstasy, and collectivism are of one and the same quality:

> Ich war die Organisatorin und Zeugin großer Taten. Ich erlebte die Geburt eines Kindes, das ein ganzes Volk mit Schweiß und Blut zur Welt brachte. Ich sah die Massen das Ende von fünfundvierzig Jahren Diktatur feiern. Ich spürte die riesigen Energien, die

> freigesetzt werden, wenn man sich traut, die Angst zu durchbrechen, mit einem Ziel, das über den einzelnen hinausgeht. Ich habe viel geweint, doch habe ich auch viel gelacht. Ich lernte die Freuden kennen, die es bedeutet, das Ich hinter sich zu lassen und das Wir zu umfangen. (Belli 2002: 11. Translation: I was the organizer and witness of exploits. I experienced the birth of a child, borne by a whole people with sweat and blood. I saw the masses celebrating the end of forty-five years of dictatorship. I felt the enormous energies that are set free when you dare to break the fear, with a goal that transcends the individual. I cried a lot, but I also laughed a lot. I got to know the pleasures that count for leaving the I behind and embracing the We.)

II.2.2 Ecstasy and Chaos

Die Stadt befand sich im Freudentaumel, einem Chaos, das manches Mal an Anarchie grenzte. (Belli 2002: 328. Translation: The city teetered in a state of ecstasy, a chaos that bordered on anarchy several times.)

It's quite obvious that to realize a revolution, a high level of energy that must be shared by a majority of the population is necessary. The revolution itself can thus be seen as the culmination point of this energy, and also as the moment when the energy that has been built up for years and maybe decades erupts. At this highest point of energy, the societal state can for sure be considered as chaotic and indeed, we are talking about the very point of system change, a moment when the course of history "suddenly begins anew, that an entirely new story, a story never known or told before, is about to unfold" (Arendt in Selbin 1999: 13). Continuing, Hannah Arendt asserts that people as the protagonists of revolution have to be convinced that with their actions, they finish with the old world order and create a completely new world.

Michele Najlis, one of the founding members of the FSLN, was very active in the Front during her youth and student life. After the 1972 earthquake, she left with her husband and son to Costa Rica, where she ended up staying until after the success of the revolution. When she came back, she described the situation as follows:

> That was our period of total euphoria. Imagine, I'd just arrived. And, naturally, in Costa Rica I'd spoken with Ernesto (Cardenal), and he'd said to be sure to be in touch when I got back. So I arrived, and you remember how things were back then: it was all

> so crazy. I couldn't even find Ernesto until someone told me he was at the Camino Real Hotel. I went out there to see him, and again it was chaos. (Najlis in Randall, 1994: 49f.)

The desire to create a totally new world and leave everything behind that belonged to the old world was built up during years of joint vision-creation, day-dreaming. On the peak of the "ritual", these dreams were followed to an irrational degree - another characteristic of Dionysus:

> I don't know if you can imagine the chaos that reigned here at the beginning. No one knew who was who. And we decided we wouldn't recognize a single document issued during the dictatorship, which of course was absurd. If the Somoza government had issued passports attesting to the fact that people were who they said they were, most likely they were. After all, they were as interested as anyone in keeping track of everyone. But we decided we had to nullify everything that came from the dictatorship. Passports were worthless, birth certificates were worthless, everything was worthless. (Najlis quoted in Randall 1994: 51)

The world had to be turned upside down, and everything that existed under the dictatorship had to be transformed into its opposite. While under the dictatorship, nobody could trust anybody, the Sandinistas decided to do the opposite, according to Michele Najlis - at least in the case of their identification: "But how were we going to figure out who was who? [...] we invented a way. It was much too complicated, but the idea behind it was beautiful: put all our trust in the people" (Najlis in Randall 1994: 51).

As we have seen in Chapter I.2 the Dionysian principle can be paralleled with the energetic principle. Ralph Abraham also connects the Dionysian with chaos and he rehabilitates the idea of chaos by saying that chaos is the essence of life (Abraham 1997).

Coming back once more to the question of social change and the role of women and men in it, I would like to highlight this urge to erase all existing structures and to allow chaos to happen as a prerequisite for the emergence of the new society. Here, it is crucial to see that there are not only external structures but that also our mind is structured according to what we've learned in our childhood and what we've internalized as roles, stereotypes, or even natural laws of evolution - all these structures that allow us to live day after day without having to question everything we do.

As important as it is to have structures that organize our minds, in the situation of society transformation, also these structures have to be broken down, because the new society has to come into being in our minds and hearts before it will materialize. Only by breaking down all the overlaying structures that our mind constructed for practical reasons, we can bring the potentials that have been suppressed but are still there to light. Then, out of the chaos, the breakthrough can happen, and a new consciousness that's necessary for the new world to come into being can emerge.

I agree with Eric Selbin who argues in his publication Modern Latin American Revolutions (1999) that it is crucial to focus on the individual persons, and not so much on the building-up process of institutions, when analyzing the ongoing societal processes in the framework of a revolution. Because the individuals are the carriers of the revolutionary energy, and without their commitment and enthusiasm, the revolution would not be possible.

> The quintessence of the social revolutionary process is the transformation of society, more specifically, of citizens. Perhaps the most eloquent and certainly the most compelling explanation of what this means was suggested to me by an older woman in Nicaragua who related with a mix of amusement, disbelief, and disgust how the wealthy in Nicaragua had treated the rest of the population as if it were 'cattle'. She hastened to assure me: 'This could never happen again. We would never allow this. We know now that we are not cattle... and we will never be their cattle again. (Selbin 1999: 4)

To tell the Nicaraguan revolution as a Dionysian ritual is helpful since it explains in a way the psychological mechanisms at work. What can be said of Dionysian rituals in ancient Greece, the dissolution of boundaries between individual and collective through the suspension of societal hierarchies, seems to be a crucial thought when talking about revolutionary uprisings as well. In this tenor, Selbin quotes Randall Collins who estimates that "The rare elation that accompanies a revolutionary uprising is probably due to there being no apparent boundary between one's own micro-situation and that prevailing anywhere else" (Collins in Selbin 1999: 13).

This quote suggests that when we talk about revolution, we are talking about a collective experience that triggers certain emotions in the participating individuals: emotions of elation and excitement or, if we translate it into a Dionysian term: energy.

I would like to follow Selbin a little bit further when he writes that "Every case of social revolution begins the period of transformation with dramatic visions" (Selbin 1999: 13). It is this vision which all out of a sudden seems to be shared by everybody, that creates this interconnectedness between the individual and the collective. Out of this, a strong personal identification with the revolutionary project can derive. The role of the individual as of utter importance to keep the system alive becomes reemphasized through the sense of communion and ownership of "their" revolution, which the individuals are likely to develop. As Daisy Zamora states:

> First of all, I want to say I've always thought that the revolution, besides belonging to the Nicaraguan people, is also my personal project. That is, it's the only thing I can really believe in and from which I expect something in return, the only thing capable of helping us build a better way of life." (Zamora in Randall 1994: 113)

On the other hand, it's exactly this personal identification, which is so necessary to keep a system in balance due to the feeling of responsibility that ideally takes hold of the individual subjects that also prevented critics to publicly voice their opinion. Especially women intellectuals tell a lot of similar stories of having been abused and treated badly by authoritative party organs – stories, which have not been told openly during the Sandinista government. The women were so personally involved in the revolutionary project, which was their own personal utopia, and for long years, the sensation of betraying their own "child", as they would call the revolution as well, if they spoke up against these obvious defects, was too strong to ignore. For sure, this behavior could also be called blind obedience to the party line for the sake of unity - an expression some of the interviewed women did use to explain their silence. This is not surprising in a country that was shaken by civil war for almost a decade, and where the military structures implemented for the revolutionary armed struggle had to be kept in place because of this. But I would still go a step further and question this "blind" obedience - especially from these strong women who knew how to express themselves through their poetry and who were aware of their intellectual capacities. It has to be emphasized once more that from a human rights point of view, people voicing their concerns or criticisms openly but in a clear and neutral manner in general didn't have to fear physical violence in the new Nicaragua. On a different level, this kind of behavior would lead to consequences, but this experience is shared by many of those women. Because within the party, some of them did voice their criticism and got silenced through forced relocation from their position or other means. But for the sake of unity, they didn't want to make even these grave injustices public. It was "their" own project that was at stake. Their interconnectedness with the project as such as well as with all the other individuals who believed in it as the realization of their own dream kept them from speaking the truth about certain structures and/or individuals abusing their power. They decided to swallow their anger for the sake of keeping the dream alive.

II.2.3 Creativity

Directly connected with the notion of chaos is the notion of creativity. Creativity is a direct result of the Dionysian energy that's also responsible for chaos. Without the energy of chaos, nothing new could emerge - thus, creativity is the force that comes out of the energy released within a Dionysian ritual. Ideally, chaos erases the old structures so that creativity can realize the "totally new world", which has been envisioned and dreamed of. It is important to see that the difficult "job" of creativity here (as a crucial driving force in the creation of the new society following revolution) is to create something new (ordering structures = Apollonian elements) without losing the balance between Dionysian (flexible, energetic) and Apollonian (ordering, form-giving) elements.

> When Tomas told me he was putting me in charge of Immigration, I said I didn't have the slightest idea what a passport was even for! All he said was, 'Me neither. No one here knows anything about anything. So go and figure it out.' And then that phrase you heard everywhere back then: 'And if you can't find out how it's done, invent something.'" (Najlis in Randall 1994: 51)

The task to "invent something" is here a strong expression of the Dionysian spirit of flexibility proven by the fact that, so it seems, everybody was given something to do and out of a total lack of standards (the only standard was that the new structure should be different from the old one), everybody was given a lot of freedom to complete his/her tasks. This proceeding seems to favor a great deal of self-responsibility, cooperation, and equality (since ideas were welcomed and considered more or less regardless from whom they came). Nobody had a recipe for the necessary tasks in the beginning, and so everybody could give his/her opinion.

One of the maybe greatest revolutionary ideas and a perfect example of Dionysian creativity (as an inherent quality of every human being: everybody can be an artist, everybody can be a piece of art) were the poetry workshops organized by the Ministry of Culture. The minister, Ernesto Cardenal, is a charismatic personality, a priest, co-founder of liberation theology, and one of the most significant Nicaraguan poets (In 2005, he was nominated for the Nobel Prize for Literature). Long before the revolution, he constructed his own utopia, when he founded a farming community sustaining itself self-sufficiently based on Christian values and organized in the form of a cooperative, where artistic forms of expression were much valued and supported. Art was considered an inherent quality of life. The painting style that was developed on the Solentiname islands where Cardenal's utopian community is based is famous for its particularity.

Following his experiences in Solentiname, as minister of culture, the poetry workshops were born out of Cardenal's heart and soul: He was completely convinced of the idea that everybody should get access to poetry. The Nicaraguans' fascination for poetry and their great poets was a procreative vehicle for this venture. Especially in times of revolution and heroic struggle, folk-poetry was blooming. Since a number of poets were in the government, the political influence of poetry was not to be underestimated. In the revolutionary state of ecstasy, the dreams were there to be realized. Gioconda Belli's poem "Warsong" is an example for this ecstatic, heroic atmosphere and shows at the same time the relational nature of this art form that connected public and private, personal and political, and emphasized the importance of interpersonal relations in the struggle:

The war will come, my love, and there will
be no truce in combat, no stopping of the
song, only poetry emerging in birth from
the dark emptied spaces of rifles. [...]
Even if we never see each other
again, even though memories will die,
I swear, because of you, I swear,
holding Nicaragua like a child to my
breast:

They will not pass, my
love, we will defeat them!
(Belli 1989: 49)

Daisy Zamora, a poet herself and vice-minister of culture under Cardenal, remembers how the atmosphere in the Ministry of Culture was a truly revolutionary one, since it was characterized by a totally different power concept:

> The whole time I was vice-minister, I don't think I ever thought of exercising power for power's sake. I don't know if I can really explain this, and of course I'm speaking in retrospect so many years later, but what's clear to me now is that Ernesto imbued the Ministry with a work-style that was profoundly revolutionary. We were truly there to serve the people, all the people; to promote a type of creativity, in which the people themselves would become the protagonists of their own cultural pageant. (Zamora in Randall 1994: 104)

But what sounded like an open and flat organization in the beginning (a flat organization could be seen as the perfect combination of Dionysian and Apollonian principles: organization is necessary for a society to function, that it should be flat would ideally mean that there are no hierarchies, which would furthermore allow creativity and Dionysian energy to flow freely), sounded different after a short time.

II.2.4 Equality

Ernesto Cardenal's brother Fernando, a priest too, realized one of the most successful campaigns of the Sandinistas aimed at equality: the literacy crusade. Thousands of young people, mainly students, joined as volunteers and went to the most remote places in the country to teach people how to read and write. The result was incredible: within two years, the illiteracy rate was reduced from more than 60 to about 15 % of the population. Gioconda Belli speaks in her autobiography of the "beeindruckendste und bewegendste aller heroischen Aktionen, die ich erleben durfte (Belli 2002: 375. Translation: most impressive and moving of all heroic activities I was allowed to experience).

Equality, especially gender equality, was one of earliest main objectives of the FSLN and it was already written down in the FSLN's 1969 historic party program. It was stated that the Sandinista revolution would "abolish the obvious discrimination that women have been subjected to compared to men [and] establish economic, political, and cultural equality between women and men" (FSLN 1969 quoted in Luciak 1998: 45). During the revolutionary struggle, women did have strong representation and they were actively participating on all levels. Women made up about 30 percent of the combatants and there were also several women commanders. In the patriarchal society of Nicaragua, the idea that women and men are fighting together for the end of the dictatorship and a different society was for sure something totally new and as such made a great impression on the people. This led the Sandinista women's association to the following optimistic comment:

> [Through the revolution] women learned in practice what we were capable of doing, and our people, without much theoretical discussion, learned what women were capable of doing. That is to say, we women didn't say we were equal - we showed it on the battlefield. On the other hand, with the taking of political power, we gained the real possibility of putting into practice the objectives of the program of the FSLN, which ... stipulated the struggle for the full emancipation of women. (AMNLAE quoted in Bayard de Volo 2001: 5)

And the Dionysian energy, the spirit of collectivism, unity, and equality combined with the ecstasy that has taken possession of so many people and of the society as a whole, paved the way for an initial glimpse of gender balance in a thoroughly patriarchal society, as the famous writer and poet Gioconda Belli tells us: "They even called me 'comandante!' But then we were all 'comandantes' back then. In that kind of atmosphere, in the euphoria of those first few months, who was going to feel discriminated against?" (Belli in Randall 1994: 176f.). Despite the revolutionary event of women and men fighting and winning the revolution together, as a team, it became very soon very clear in the aftermath of the revolution that this new alliance was not going to be continued in the same path. After the initial chaos, governmental structures were put into place in the new Nicaragua, and at that point it can be observed how women were, again, missing in the decision-making bodies. Zamora explains how she experienced the Dionysian energy of collectivism and equality, and the total disruption of the old structures as a woman:

> It's absolutely true that the revolution opened up a new space for women here. We fought alongside our male comrades and that produced an explosion of new possibilities. By the end of the war, the old order had been completely disrupted, and all the women who had taken part had the opportunity of working in our

> respected fields to help construct a more just society. I think the problem was that this new space wasn't accompanied by a new mentality on the part of most of the male-dominated leadership. (Zamora in Randall 1994: 111)

This resistance on the male side to accept any different power model than the old, hierarchical, patriarchal one created a structural inequality right from the beginning. It should take the FSLN until 1994 to include women in the national directorate, which is considered the most important party-internal decision-making body.

On the other hand, these shortcomings didn't stop women from being active designers of their country in the first place. Especially in the early 1980's, they seemed to embrace the opportunity to create a new society by peaceful means, as we can read in Bayard de Volo:

> Toward its goal of economic, political, and cultural equality for women, the FSLN abolished prostitution, banned advertising that exploited women's bodies, instituted equal pay for equal work, provided health care for mothers and children, built day-care centers, and expanded literacy. AMNLAE and some FSLN leaders asserted that men must share a larger part of domestic tasks and child care. Women not only benefited from these objectives but also played a primary role in carrying them out. They constituted 60 percent of the literacy brigades, 70 percent of the brigades for the popular health campaign, 95 percent of those working in health programs, and 68 percent of the coordinators in adult education programs. (Bayard de Volo 2001: 35f.)

In all these campaigns that had a long-term effect on all the Nicaraguan people, women constituted a majority. So, while in their country, the Sandinistas did implement a strong sense of equality and emancipation of women by leaving the deepest structural changes in their hands, it seems that in their own "family", in the highest circles of power, they failed to include women right from the beginning. We could say the Sandinista nuclear family was discriminating against women, while its mass organizations were celebrating them. Since the nuclear family is the core element of a societal system, this contradiction had to yield fruit, sooner or later.

It shall only be noted here that this failure of the male Sandinista leaders to include women in their leadership circles, or in other words, in their symbolic nuclear family, was reflected in the real nuclear families all over the country: here is the place, it seems, where the Sandinista ideals of freedom and equality stopped: so far and no further.

II.3 The "New Nicaragua" as a Transrational System

> The larger picture that emerges indicates that all the modern, post-Enlightenment movements for social justice, be they religious or secular, as well as the more recent feminist, peace, and ecology movements, are part of an underlying thrust for the transformation of a dominator to a partnership system. (Eisler 1988: xx)

II.3.1 How did the System work?

It is maybe the most telling part of this book that I couldn't write this chapter. It is almost a pervading line through the interviews and reports that in the memories of many Nicaraguans, 1985 was a turning point (for example Najlis in Randall 1994: 56). Without referring to any specific event, this is the tenor of most of the witnesses: In 1985, things started to change. Without being an expert on the historical events that took place in each and every year of Sandinista leadership in the country, I started to feel uneasy about this mythical year. Why 1985? What happened? What was before, and what was afterwards?

What stands out is that some time in 1985, the Sandinista period reached half of its time. Could it be that this is the landmark witnesses, contemporaries, Nicaraguans set after the electoral defeat of their FSLN, a landmark they needed to figure out what happened? Could it be that this date, 1985, was used from more and more former revolutionary activists, reading it in one interview, in another book, from one another? And that, in the end, 1985 constituted a myth - the mythological time when things started to change, when the Apollonian started to take over again, when collective optimism was replaced by individual pessimism?

What does all this have to do with my problems to write a chapter on the functioning of the system of the new Nicaragua? When I developed the structural framework for this case study, I was of the opinion, that the revolution must be structured as such: initially, there must have been a period of ecstasy, euphoria, and collectivity - the Dionysian ritual. That was the time of the revolutionary struggle, its success and its chaotic, creative aftermath. Sooner or later, order must have been brought into the picture again, but it was different from how it was before: power was seen differently, hierarchies were flat, everybody could say something and was listened to, equality, freedom, human rights, education and health service for everybody. I thought this was the period when the system was in balance: when the female and the male, the Dionysian and the Apollonian aspects of human nature were honored in kind. And finally, there must have been the time of breakdown... the balance was shattered by an Apollonian force becoming stronger and stronger, and slowly the old structures of power over instead of power for, of competition instead of cooperation with its consequences: corruption, violence etc. came into place again.

In the end, it seems to show that this ideal, Apollonian kind of three part structure is not there. Finally, I would rather suggest a new view on my own ideas and come to the point, that quite likely, there was never a balance, really. Rather, there was the time of Dionysian predominance that was the time of the ritual, the collectivist experience, ecstasy and euphoria. As Nietzsche suggests, after every Dionysian ritual, sooner or later there comes the rude awakening (comparable to a hangover after excessive drinking, for instance). In this new analysis, the symbol of 1985 symbolizes this awakening; and after the awakening, a "going back to normal" is likely, as Bayard de Volo puts it:

> Did the revolutionary process produce images of women that might enlarge the arena of opportunities for women, as FSLN discourse proposed? On the contrary, despite women's revolutionary experience and the FSLN's considerable effort to improve women's economic position, the contra-war, along with a revolutionary party not fully committed to feminist ideals, led to a regression back to the safer, traditional images and roles for women. Crossing gender boundaries during exceptional circumstances, such as popular insurrection, did not secure women an equal position in the 'New Society', nor did it fundamentally alter traditional notions of femininity. During the post-triumph euphoria, visions of fundamental social change, including equal rights for women, competed with a popular yearning to return to normalcy, especially within the home. With the enemy defeated, the 'guerrilla girls' could lay down their weapons, return home, and bear and raise children in a new, revolutionary society. (Bayard de Volo 2001: 38)

This quotation shows what is "normal" in our understanding: A dominator system, men dominating women, rich dominating poor, powerful dominating powerless.

II.3.2 Why did the System collapse? A Feminist Interpretation.

> I think a lot of it had to do with the fact that the FSLN took power through armed struggle, with the almost military structure that implies. And those very vertical chains of command remained in place. The intensification of the Contra war also favored maintaining those structures; it favored, but in my opinion, didn't justify them. (Najlis in Randall 1994: 56)

Najlis continues by saying that in the war zones, in the military ranks the hierarchical order was necessary, but that she couldn't see a reason for the adoption of the same strict structures in the political life of the capital Managua. It is almost obvious that the "chain of command" Najlis talks about had a great deal to do with the problems that became more and more visible within the movement and affected also the rest of the country.

Gioconda Belli adds another interesting observation that sheds a new light on the celebrated and glorified revolutionary ideals. In her point of view, the change from a Dionysian to an Apollonian model didn't happen gradually, after the revolutionary success and with the intensification of the Contra war. On the contrary, she states:

> (A)s soon as victory began to seem like a possibility, things began to change. It's not true that things changed after the war ended; they began to change before. For example, I remember in June of 1979, when the tendencies reunited[11] and they began to organize different groups of comrades to carry out different tasks, all the leaders were men. I complained. I remember how I protested; I said, 'I've been in charge here for a while, I've been responsible for this group. Why is a man suddenly being put in charge?' No one even bothered to give me an answer. [...] What I'm saying is that

[11] In the years before the victory, the FSLN was divided into three different tendencies: the GPP - Prolonged Popular War wing, the Proletarian Tendency and the wing of the "Terceristas", the third or pragmatic faction. This split was perceived as endangering the whole revolutionary project for a while, but finally the tendencies mixed up more or less in the fights and later constituted a political party including the leaders of all three factions.

> we didn't analyze the discrimination at the time. We felt we had gotten what we wanted, by being allowed to fight. And you have to remember, everything was very chaotic, very intense. But in retrospect it's quite clear; the moment victory became a possibility, that's when we women who had been active participants in the struggle began to be forced out, to lose power, to be marginalized. We'd been on the front lines, and then we weren't. (Belli in Randall 1994: 176)

Individual interests of almost exclusively men who felt powerful and thus executed their power in a very traditional, patriarchal way, started to corrupt the noble ideals of the revolution. The story of Daisy Zamora tells how she lost her job because of being committed to her service for the people and to the revolutionary principles she believed in and how individual vanities destroyed an important part of the revolutionary self-conception of Nicaragua: the poetry workshops. "It's just that I believed that the revolution had a cultural project; and when that project came up against certain individuals' personal ambition, the problems became insoluble" (Zamora in Randall 1994: 105). The collectivist cultural project of the revolution was fast enough threatened by interests of individuals. Zamora was one of the people who dared to challenge those individuals who considered themselves more powerful and important than the collectivist ideals. After she was forced to leave the Ministry of Culture, she was sent to jobs connected to party administration as a penalty, where rigid discipline was ruling. In her analysis of her own and her superior's behavior, she explains how she came to commit herself to a different vision of power, one that was connected to responsibility rather than dominance.

> (O)f course, I didn't last long in either place because I continued to open my mouth when I had something to say. It wasn't that I always thought I was right; I just couldn't stand this 'correct line', where there was a single vision, a single right way of doing things, without any recognition at all of the possibility of error. Maintaining a democratic process seemed important to me. (Zamora in Randall 1994: 106)

Zamora called the continuous attacks against the ministry's most ideological activity, the poetry workshops for everybody, the biggest conflict. In her record, the wrangling over the workshops appears as motivated by personal power struggles. This was the end of the ideal, and Zamora's words are full of sorrow and disappointment:

> The poetry workshops weren't conceived of only so people who wanted to write poetry would have a place to do so. They were an attempt to get people to read poetry, too, and to understand that creativity belongs to us all; we have only to tap it. But the experiment, which I believe was a profoundly revolutionary one - one that retrieved the most important cultural tradition we have here, which is poetry - became an object of continual attack, until the workshops ceased to exist.
>
> These personal vendettas shouldn't have been allowed to flourish within the revolution. No one person, just because he or she liked you or didn't like you or wanted your job or had some personal motive for attack, should ever have been able to destroy a revolutionary project like that. (Zamora in Randall 1994: 107)

Of course, there is no perfect society in the sense that personal interests would seize to exist. But at the same time, these early abuses of power as something that belonged to individuals and that could be used against other individuals had its consequences. According to Veronika Kauffmann, "(i)n a static hierarchic system, dynamic energy is trapped" (Kauffmann 1997). The natural flow of the energy seemed to be blocked, and Najlis observed painfully how a certain level of corruption developed in the leadership. This closed the circle and brought the traditional power concept, connected to a hierarchical and patriarchal society organization back into place.

> I won't say all the leaders became corrupt, but too many did. And this, too, tended to support the verticality of the state and the Party - because if you have someone who's corrupt at the top, he's naturally not going to permit criticism from the bottom. [...] From 1985 on, we began to see this sort of problem. (Najlis in Randall 1994: 56)

Najlis narrates how she never had problems of respect despite her being a woman with the people working under her; but how she almost from the beginning was not taken serious by the men above her. It is an especially interesting part of her story how she identifies Daniel Ortega, who got re-elected president of Nicaragua in 2006, as "one of the worst" regarding disrespect and ignorance towards women and their specific problems.

> I remember the day Daniel said something about abortion being "one of those exotic ideas imported from Europe and the United States." He said it was something only intellectuals were concerned about, that it didn't have any relevance in the lives of ordinary people. Doctors at the Berta Calderôn Hospital told him, "Comandante, two hundred fifty women a year die of botched abortions in this hospital alone. And that's not counting those who never make it to the hospital." But he kept insisting it was "intellectual claptrap." The same for family planning; he didn't want to hear about it. (Najlis quoted in Randall 1994: 57)

The fascination of the Nicaraguan revolution captured many intellectuals around the world. Maybe this is the reason that these alarming stories about the then- and today-president of Nicaragua are usually not considered in the several critical articles in - mainly leftist - western media about the re-election of a man, who seems to have lost his revolutionary ideals somewhere on the way from the defeat in 1990 to his re-election in 2006. This loss is regretted tremendously but the initial problems caused by Ortega's traditional world view are not mentioned. It seems that the utopia had to be perfect, the hope had to be kept alive and the only harmful influx in Nicaragua was the bad US imperialism. Wolfgang Dietrich calls this attitude an "Apollonian neurosis" of the west (Dietrich 2006b). Ortega's rigid stance on abortion then appears to be a big surprise and disappointment:

> Jüngste Ergebenheitsgeste gegenüber dem Klerus war der von Rosario Murillo angeführte Kreuzzug gegen die medizinisch indizierte Abtreibung. Seit der Regierung des liberalen Präsidenten José Santos Zelaya im Jahr 1891 ist der Schwangerschaftsabbruch straffrei, wenn die Mutter gefährdet oder die Schwangerschaft auf Vergewaltigung zurückzuführen ist. Eine Woche vor den Wahlen peitschte das Parlament mit den sandinistischen Stimmen eine Gesetzesnovelle durch, die jede Form der Abtreibung unter Strafe für Mutter und Arzt stellt. (Leonhard 2006: 14. Translation: The most recent gesture of devotion towards the clergy was the crusade against medically referred abortion led by Rosario Murillo. Since the rule of liberal president José Santos Zelaya in 1891 abortion is legal, if the mother is endangered or if the pregnancy is a consequence of rape. One week before the elections the parliament

> pushed through an amendment that makes all forms of abortion a punishable offence for the mother and the doctor).

The German *Linkszeitung* laments under the poetic title *How the Revolution Sold Its Soul* about the final loss of the FSLN's progressive political positions: "Die Führung der Frente opferte damit endgültig wichtige progressive Positionen und passt sich an die voraufklärerische Realität Nicaraguas an. Eine ehemals starke Stimme für Gleichberechtigung, Aufklärung und Laizismus ist so verloren gegangen" (Schützhofer 2007. Translation: The leadership of the Frente sacrifices therewith ultimately important progressive positions and adapts to the pre-enlightenment reality of Nicaragua. A formerly strong voice for equality, enlightenment and laicism has thus gotten lost).

Najlis also excoriates the FSLN's women's organization AMNLAE. We learn that AMNLAE was "simply an appendage of the FSLN, run by male members of the national directorate who frequently made terrible comments about women and women's issues" (Najlis quoted in Randall 1994: 57).

A different view on AMNLAE is given by Bayard de Volo. She is telling the story of AMNLAE's struggle for equal duties, not rights, for women in the Contra war . In 1983, with the intensification of the contra attacks, the FSLN proposed a draft for all 17- to 25-year-old men. They should be called for a 2-year compulsory military service. While this regulation should earn huge criticism in the coming years especially from the mothers' movement Mothers of Heroes and Martyrs, led by mothers of fallen Sandinistas who wanted the government to stop taking their sons to the mountains, AMNLAE was in the beginning opposing the idea of having a draft only for men:

> AMNLAE argued that the participation of women in combat during the insurrection had most effectively altered society's conception of women's capabilities. Furthermore, to the extent that military defense was seen as the duty, even the privilege, of male citizens, prominent members of AMNLAE argued that this should be applied to women too. They were also concerned that military discrimination could lead to other forms as well, thus impeding the FSLN's 1969 goal of abolishing discrimination against women. A common refrain was, 'Women have earned the right in Nicaragua to participate in the defense of the country.' Accordingly, AMNLAE pushed for full integration of women into all tasks of

> the revolution, including the draft, as essential to gender equality. The FSLN leadership countered that social services, particularly day care, were insufficient; thus women were needed at home to care of their children. (Bayard de Volo 2001: 36)

This argument shows how times had changed back in 1983: The women have found their mission, they are great in non-violent, civil society activities, there are perfect for the different revolutionary campaigns (the literacy crusade, the health crusade etc.), but fighting should be left for men. This imbalance didn't only exclude women from the military as a matter of fact, but it also changed the nature of the military and of the male revolutionary fighter. Insofar as it strengthened stereotypical gender roles, the party line provoked almost naturally the collapse of the system. There was a total failure to understand the need to transform the existing, unequal gender relations completely and instead, the same structures that were in place in the traditional patriarchal family were simply reproduced . If we take Elise Boulding's metaphor of a societal system as a household where every member has to be respected and treated with dignity, we can easily see how this way of treating women in the "household" of the FSLN did not support society transformation towards these values. The almost autocratic leadership circle of the FSLN, the *National Directorate,* didn't include any female members, which makes its dealing with their own female partners in the revolutionary project maybe a bit more comprehensible. But we learn that, although it seems hard to believe, the same revolution which was realized by "poets and authors" over time came to also limit the spheres of action of its own creative potential: its artists. After the Ministry of Culture led by Ernesto Cardenal has been closed, the *Institute of Culture* was founded and went, headed by Daniel Ortega's wife Rosario Murrillo, into a totally different direction. Now, the artists were not asked about their opinions anymore; an autocratic structure was finally put in place to "organize" what I would like to call the "nuclear motivation system" of a society in its transformation process towards partnership and equality: its artists. Najlis, an artist herself, tells about the peaceful protest some of the artists decided to stage. The reaction was a thoroughly violent one, aimed to shut down every kind of criticism from the inside of the Party. Unconditional, military obedience was demanded.

> They summoned us to a meeting with Tomas (Borge), Sergio (Ramirez), and Daniel (Ortega). [...] Those men said terrible things to us that day: that we were fence sitters, that the first to

> desert the revolution would be its artists and writers, things like that. [...] The hostility was systematic. As artists, we had become undesirables. As women, well, we were appendages. [...] Those attitudes were part of a whole leadership style, and you began to find that style everywhere you looked. (Najlis quoted in Randall 1994: 58)

Being offered a Hobson's choice, most of the artists were not ready to leave the party for the sake of freedom of opinion. It is indeed a hard decision to take: what was asked of them was to leave the love of their lives, their revolution, just because some ignorant autocratic men thought they were the owners of what was once a movement of the masses that belonged to everybody. So, even the most critical intellectuals were shocked facing the loss of the elections in 1990. The pain was unimaginable: as we learn from Najlis, she and many other women and artists had all the time hoped that they were wrong in their assessment, that in the end, the ideal would win. The last election campaign "didn't really say anything. [...] But no, I didn't think we were going to lose. It saddened me, but I thought we'd win. And then, when we did lose, my world fell apart" (Najlis quoted in Randall 1994: 59).

II.2.2.1"Quien te quiere, te aporrea."[12] The Role of Machismo

Roger N. Lancaster's anthropological study about the people in the new Nicaragua traces the roots of this shortcoming. He finds them by defining machismo as a system of power relations.

> In others words, under machismo, relations between men, women, and children are structured in certain standard ways. Moreover, what it is to properly be a man, or a woman, or a child, is also defined relationally, within the logic of the system. These relations themselves - not their idealized representation or coarse expression - constitute the system of machismo. (Lancaster 1992: 20)

The way Lancaster describes the system of machismo clearly identifies it as a dominator system. As he states, too, its transformation into a partnership system is by no means easy and therefore he doesn't seem surprised about its ostensible failure:

---

[12] The one who loves you, beats you. Old Nicaraguan Proverb, quoted in Lancaster 1992: 34.

> Because systems function as systems, operating by and reproducing their own logic - no less in the personalities of people than in the realm of international commerce - the relations they engender are not easily redefined, even by deliberate, self-conscious efforts. [...] Genders, sexualities, and bodies thus produced also silently, imperceptibly reproduce the logic of the system - even when its obvious inequalities are under challenge. (Lancaster 1992: 20)

I would consider this a very important remark, which Lancaster proves with a number of examples from his own experiences. He tells of a young couple, both Sandinistas, she a feminist, both determined to represent the "new Man" and "new Woman" of Nicaragua[13]. They live together, she gets a baby, everything seems perfect until the young man has to travel more and more for his job. In the end, she has to realize that he had a relationship in every city he traveled to frequently, and fathered some more children. Although both were conscious about the inequalities in the traditional society and committed to live an alternative, in the end, they couldn't escape the system. Lancaster emphasizes, that this system traps both and not only the woman, although she is clearly seen as the victim of this unbalanced relationship:

> Machismo as a system trades in innumerable risks and dangers: some physical, others psychological. In the culture of machismo, as in any system of power, people are compelled to manoeuver their way through its available options. A woman is always at some risk in this system: she might be beaten, she might be abandoned. A man has more options but is no less at risk. In a context where the burdens of manhood weigh heavily, he might fail to maintain an appropriate masculinity. (Lancaster 1992: 198)

To find the balance between the requirements of the "new Man" and the kind of behavior that is requested by a man to maintain his masculinity must have created an identity crisis in many young Nicaraguan men - especially with a war going on, where the hero archetype was still in place

[13] The term "New Man" was coined by Che Guevara in 1965. In his article "El socialismo y el hombre en Cuba" he expressed the need to change human beings as such and not only society. He described the "New Man" (he used the term in its male form) as "without greed, open, generous of spirit, filled with solidarity towards those less fortunate than himself, and capable of generating and living by more human values." (Randall 1992: 2)

and earning its credit. One of the essential assets of the masculine hero is his virility (remember the innocent little song of the young revolutionary in the mountains Vidaluz Meneses told us about). The consequences are fragile and unstable family relations; legal marriages are rare in Nicaragua, especially in the lower classes. It's much more common to just live together in an informal way. It's very common for men to just leave and start a new family somewhere else. But this is not a result of the casual way sexual relationships are handled, as Lancaster states. On the contrary, this irresponsible behavior of men is a direct consequence of the system of machismo.

> It might seem that the informal character of cohabitation contributes to the brittleness of unions in Nicaragua, and perhaps that is so. Without a tradition of formal and legal constraints, men do abandon women and children to start new families. It might even be argued that this arrangement facilitates the irresponsible sexual behavior of men. But informal union as an institution occurs in the context of the culture of machismo, not vice versa." (Lancaster 1992: 45)

Margaret Randall adds a key thought to this description of paternal failures: The current family structures in Nicaragua developed in the framework of patriarchal values imposed by the Spanish colonizers and deepened through the imposition of capitalist economic structures. "This type of agro-capitalist development, imposed by the United States, brought with it the exploitative social structures needed to keep it in place. These regulate the family and affect women in particularly debilitating ways" (Randall 1994: 13).

One woman explains why women in Nicaragua mostly prefer not to marry:

> Because Nicaraguan men are such machistas. They think they can beat their wives and do whatever else they please. And this is a Catholic country, so it's very difficult to get a divorce; it's virtually unheard of. And anyway, most women believe it's a terrible sin to get a divorce: they think you'll go to hell for that. So when a woman marries a man, she's agreeing to put up with whatever he decides to do. This isn't good for women. It's much better, much more sensible, to live with him without a church wedding. That way, if he tries to beat you, you can leave him, or if he takes up with other women, you can get out of it, or at least you can threaten to leave. (Dona Celia quoted in Lancaster 1992: 46)

With the revolution and its ideals, the traditional image of the Nicaraguan macho was, as I already mentioned, put into question - at least on the superficial level. Men couldn't deny that women had proven to be capable of a lot more than staying home and raising kids when they fought side by side with them in the guerrilla, and at the same time, women's emancipation was a clear-cut goal of the FSLN from the beginning. As a movement for social change, equality and justice, gender equality was naturally part of the vision of the future. As Randall puts it:

> Paternal irresponsibility remains a fundamental problem. It is one that the Sandinista administration attempted to deal with throughout its decade in office. Exploitative economies have traditionally made it difficult for men to earn a decent wage, and their resulting depression, along with patriarchal attitudes situating women as objects of use and abuse, conspire in leading many men to abandon their legal or free-union wives and young children. (Randall 1994: 13)

In 1988, 20-year-old Jaime reports the changes he sees in the stereotypical male-female dichotomy, referring to the revolutionary "New Man":

> These ideas have changed a lot, and are still changing, since the revolution. Some people have the old ideal; other people have the new one, so it's hard to say. The new idea of a good man - that is, the revolutionary New Man - is someone who studies to improve himself and his country, who works hard, who is responsible towards his companera, his children, and is generous with those around him. The old idea of the good man - the ideal of machismo - was someone who could drink, fight, gamble, and have a large number of sexual conquests. It was as simple as that. (Lancaster 1992: 175)

The difficulty of the new time was, so Jaime, that there was a lot of confusion among young men and boys about the transition from the old to the new paradigm. There were some men (mostly the older generation, for example their fathers) who still lived according to the old ideal, but also other men in their immediate environment (mostly the younger generation, for example their older brothers) who tried to realize an alternative manhood. So the new generation of men had different models to follow, which automatically leads to confusion. We can roughly compare this situation to the identity crisis male youth face in our western societies today, where the "New Man" also keeps appearing for years in public debate but the prototype of the traditional man is still very present - not only in the homes, but especially as a role model in the media. Different from the situation in the west, the transformation of manhood in Nicaragua can be seen as something that seemed to develop much faster and abrupt than we could ever imagine. As a starting point, there was a strong machismo culture in place that can only be understood as a prototype of a patriarchal dominator culture, where men acted solely following their own desires (this can absolutely be understood in a sexual e.g. sexist sense), without much sense for responsibility and caring. The transformation of this deeply rooted identity into its opposite therefore was maybe the most difficult part in the general transformation process of the Nicaraguan society. Especially in a situation where military ideals had to be kept alive, and heroes and martyrs were honored and praised as there seemed no other way to keep the population on rather supportive tracks concerning the Contra war and the numerous sacrifices it demanded, the project of changing the ideal of manhood seems incredibly difficult. So we read in the testimonials of witnesses how even those men who were consciously committing themselves to become "New Men" at times fell back into severe macho behavior.

> And clearly, some people have changed more than others. For instance, you now have men who help out around the house. This was unthinkable before. No man would be caught washing dishes or cooking or ironing. [...] But now many mothers are rearing their sons with the expectation that they're supposed to help out around the house. And now, with so many women working, women are saying, 'Look, it's not fair that I work on a job the same as you and then come home and do all the work at the house.' And with the new ideas about cooperation between men and women, there are more and more men who help with the housework and children. Nevertheless, some of these same men sometimes have lapses and do something very machista. (Lancaster 1992: 176)

Another young man, 17-year-old Roger, shared his thoughts about the storied "New Man". His statement is a direct pointer to the very nature of this project: it was an attempt to transform a society that was based on Apollonian individualism to a society directed towards Dionysian collectivism: Interview with Roger, a 17-year-old high school student:

> At the same time, there is no 'New Man' - only talk of him, and little pieces of him here and there. We are no doubt closer to this

> collectivist idea than before. But the egoist remains very strong. Many kids my age are concerned about nothing but shirts, pants, how they look, and a lot of them just want to breakdance all day. (Lancaster 1992: 148)

The collectivist idea also prevailed when parents had to bury their fallen sons. One father held a speech at his son's wake: "My son was a good boy, a conscientious man. It is tragic that he lost his life this way, but this is a tragedy that we share with all Nicaraguan families, and we know that he is protected in the love of God. His death will not be in vain" (Lancaster 1992: 200f.).

As Nietzsche rephrased the consoling message of Dionysianism as "individuals come and go, but the chorus will always be there", the collective spirit of defending what was the dream and vision of so many people seems to make place for a consoling message too, confronted with the death of family members: as long as the struggle goes on, as long as our revolution is still there, the loss of individuals has a purpose.

But at some point, it seems, this spirit has been lost... Gioconda Belli tells about her interpretation of the fatal role machismo played in the new Nicaragua:

> (I)n a way, I feel we lost the revolution to a form of political machismo. Our men felt powerful, and they stood before the world like gorillas banging their breasts. The pride in what they had been able to do, the war they had won, that was most important to them. They felt powerful, invincible. And everyday life, the common concerns of common people - including the situation of women - they just weren't interested." (Belli in Randall 1994: 188)

Belli goes on to analyze the failures of the Party leaders, but also their "followers" like herself who didn't speak up in time against those power struggles that left the people outside, hungry, and poor. Recognizing her own responsibility for not having made herself heard in public, she opts for a different model, a real society transformation.

> Having lived through an experience like this sobers you, believe me. It makes you realize how unacceptable it is that your individuality be subordinated to some notion of 'truth' that you are supposed to accept against all reason and sensitivity. Subjectivity is valid; it must nurture collective thought. After all, collective ideas are born in individual minds; and often, behind the defense

> of the 'correct interpretation', there's a power struggle going on to see whose subjectivity will prevail. So, the reformulation of the same project of social justice I talked about before, the same project we attempted and failed to bring off because of this political machismo, has to be based in real democracy, in an authentic struggle to achieve consensus, in people's participation not in feats of war but in the solving of everyday problems. (Belli in Randall 1994: 189)

Finally, she makes a strong point for a partnership model based on the values of care and relation women represent best, and for a society based on energetic peace, including flexibility and creativity.

> I think we women are particularly well suited for this task. But the problem is that the models we are forced to use are based on moral decisions reached through deductions from principles and not drawn from the real interaction that takes place in real life among real people. If you operate from a principle of care, based on real needs that must be met and not on some notion of patriotism or Party loyalty, you'll be in a much better position to start solving the problems of misery, hunger, and underdevelopment. Women have been operating from a principle of care for most of our history. We are trained to care for and nurture others. And instead of seeing this as a handicap - much like our capacity for giving birth has been turned into a handicap - we should be able to generate and socialize a new kind of ethic, new rules of the game. (Belli in Randall 1994: 189f.)

II.3.2.2 Promiscuity

> Looking back, this all seems like some sort of golden age in that respect. Women participated to an extraordinary degree, and there were a number of women who had positions of real responsibility. But there is one thing: there was sexual promiscuity. Not a whole lot, but some. And you know that in our society this always affects women's lives much more than it does men's. It was accepted that a comrade would have an affair, and then another, and another. They justified it by saying that since any one of us might be killed at any time, we had to live our lives as intensely as possible. And then, too, there was the mobility; you slept one night here, another there, for reasons of safety. That life-style, with its ever-present

> dangers, generates its own dynamic. This is the only thing I couldn't quite reconcile myself to, as a woman. (Belli in Randall 1994: 175)

This statement of Gioconda Belli expresses, in my opinion, one of the core problems of the Sandinista revolution. As has been made clear in the previous chapter, is the Nicaraguan traditional society characterized by a culture of machismo, which gives men a lot more rights than women, particularly also in the sense of sexual freedoms. When young women who were traditionally "protected" by their fathers or older brothers in the name of her (and the family's) honor started to participate in the liberation struggle, went underground etc., these women developed a new feeling of control over their bodies, and what took place there can clearly be understood as some kind of sexual revolution (as Belli stated, in the omnipresent danger of losing one's life, the day had to be lived). The collectivist experience of the revolution itself, as a Dionysian ritual, where borders between individual and collective were broken down, gender or social status didn't play a role and communal ecstasy was there, can be understood as an atmosphere, which stimulated a sexual liberation of both women and men.

But we already found, too, that the change of consciousness, the total disruption of the old order did not happen in the homes, in the private spaces, due to a lack of awareness in the Sandinista leadership and maybe due to the short time these new ideas had to settle into each and every member of the system. What Belli means when she talks about how women's lives are affected by this kind of promiscuity, therefore, is exactly this discrepancy between the superficial atmosphere of equality, collectivism and creativity and the traditional understanding of gender roles in the home, in the nuclear families.

In this context, stories of gender discrimination and devaluation of women as objects like Daisy Zamora's should be understood. Zamora tells how she was punished politically for ending her marriage with a minister of state and living with a progressive man who was considered "controversial", and later for being punished even more for rejecting a powerful man who wanted sex with her, one of the "comandantes". "What I'm saying is that not being willing to go to bed with that kind of power broker not only cost me my own power niche, it prevented me from finding work" (Zamora in Randall 1994: 110). All these experiences led her to a deeper understanding of the political processes going on around her, and she developed a truly revolutionary vision of power.

> All of this has led to my profound belief that we need a totally different conception of power, one that includes a truly humanist, feminist perspective. And when I talk about a feminist perspective, I'm not talking only about so-called women's issues: I mean a different conception of the world, of relations between people, of power relations on all levels. (Zamora in Randall 1994: 110)

Because this treatment of her as a female intellectual loyal to the revolutionary goals could only take place because of the imbalanced society structure based on unequal gender relations. "In the eyes of a number of our male leaders, women continued to be seen as 'meat' or 'cattle,' as our macho slang would have it. The quickest and easiest way for political women to acquire a 'protector' and gain direct access to power was by sleeping with someone in power" (Zamora in Randall 1994: 109). Since Zamora dared to refuse such an offer, she had to suffer deeply.

Milú Vargas, another Sandinista intellectual, has another impressive story of discrimination on the basis of gender to tell. When she was considered to become a member of the FSLN, she had already started a relationship with one of the members of the national directorate, Carlos Nunez Tellez. He was separated from his wife but still married to her, and Vargas was the one who was blamed and punished politically for that thing still considered outrageous in a strictly catholic society. The fact that nobody considered the man responsible she explains with the factors sex and power. But instead of letting him intervene on her behalf, she was willing to fight it through, for herself and for all the other women who suffered discrimination in the party on different levels. She considers this an important time in her relationship (since it gave them the chance to discuss issues of gender and discrimination), for the struggle of the women's movement and for understanding processes of social change in general:

> You know, I think a central problem with this sort of thing is when you begin to separate the private and public spheres, to make different rules for each. We tend to look at our political leaders one way in terms of their public image and quite another in the context of their private lives. We forget it's the same person. And so there's a problem of coherence. The richness of multi-layered experiences is lacking. When we think of revolution only in terms of economics, agrarian reform, literacy, state-controlled industry and

> the rest, when we think of revolution only in terms of external and not internal change, I think we fail to go as deep as we must. (Vargas in Randall 1994: 133)

In a system, every single part has to be changed to really achieve systems change. In Nicaragua, the "wind of change" has touched a great number of people, a huge majority of individuals, but the understanding of the profoundness of this change, that it has to go under the skin and affect the minds and hearts of everybody - this realization was maybe the most important missing link. And it was missing because the outstanding personalities who really made the incredible happen, who really led the revolution to triumph, lacked this understanding personally. Vargas analyses this lack of awareness in a very concrete way:

> (T)he Party never adequately addressed the political aspects of so-called private conduct. We never reflected on this, not collectively in any case. Personal conduct was seen in a moralistic way, if it was seen at all, and that was a big mistake. Because change comes about only as a result of perceived necessity. If we recognize our need to have more complete relationships, a fuller and more integrated life, that's what pushes us to change. (Vargas in Randall 1994: 133)

But this "mistake", as Vargas calls it, had serious consequences: with the separation between public and private life kept in place, the old dualistic world order prevailed, speaking of the system as a whole. Still, men were not allowed to be weak or to express feelings, still women were not really taken serious in politics or at least their bodies were seen as inferior and therefore objects for male usage as Zamora has depicted it so impressively. The consequence of this failure was a grave one. Vargas brings it down to the point: "(W)e have plenty of men who do excellent jobs in their public political life but who have very abusive relations with their wives and children" (Vargas in Randall 1994: 133). Zamora's poem of a *Loyal Housewife* is a bloodcurdling document about a woman's role in post-revolutionary Nicaragua:

Everything ended with the
Honeymoon: the orange blossoms, the
love letters, the childish weeping.

Now you crawl at your master's feet, first in his harem, taken or
abandoned according to his will. Mother of children who bear his
name, bemoaning your lot beside a clothesline heavy with diapers,
wringing your heart until it is purified in sheets and towels.
Accustomed to the shouts, the humiliation
of a hand held out for crumbs. A woman
cornered, a plaintive shadow, suffering
migraines, varicose veins, diabetes.

A young girl kept for show who married her
first boyfriend and grew old listening to the
distant song of life
from her place of wifely honor.

(Zamora 1993: 65)

II.3.3 The Aftermath: Emerging Consciousness

After Michele Najlis' world fell apart, she realized that she had been right all the time: the revolution was lost, the party had turned itself upside down and the old, hierarchical order of the dominator society had been put into place again. The revolution had empowered her and a great number of Nicaraguans tremendously: they realized that the future is in their own hands, and that it's up to every single individual to change it for the better. This is an amazingly big step towards society transformation. Milú Vargas confirms this by giving credit to the revolution, which only made it possible for the women to realize the gender inequalities that were there.

> You know, I consider this a real gift. The FSLN enabled us to grow to the extent that we were able to claim autonomy, think for ourselves, create new alternatives and new possibilities of struggle. I believe we women are an important part of the Front's rich history. Because if the Front had enabled us only to mimic what we heard, if it had kept us down - incapable of creating anything new - then it wouldn't have been much of a political organization. Our experience in the FSLN is what gave us this strength, this possibility for change. (Vargas in Randall 1994: 140)

When Najlis illustrates what had happened to her personally, it seems that only after the electoral defeat, another kind of consciousness could take over, has been set free: the feminist consciousness: "I'm forty-five, and since I was thirteen and fourteen years old I've been accustomed to thinking of myself as a subject of history, not an object. Actually, I used to think of myself as *un sujeto*. Now I think of myself as *una sujeta"* (Najlis in Randall 1994: 62).

It seems that after the FSLN's unexpected electoral defeat in 1990, the feminist movement in Nicaragua could finally develop free of party or other constraints. The Contra war was finally declared over, but instead, the country was immediately faced with a lot of new challenges: new laws like the prohibition of homosexuality and severe cutbacks in social services. As Vargas put it, "Women are no longer going to defend the country as our first priority. We are going to defend women as our first priority. That means fighting for the right to abortion and against violence" (Vargas in Bayard de Volo 2001: 163).

For the feminist movement to speak up in public, it can be argued that the electoral defeat of the FSLN was very important. Only after this unexpected and painful loss, the women involved with feminist ideas realized how they had refrained from making their voices heard in public during all those years. This refusal to accept and express a reality cannot be seen in the framework of party loyalty only. As we saw, the myth of motherhood is deeply rooted in the Nicaraguan culture. It was Gioconda Belli whose words I used to explain how the revolution was seen as a collectivist struggle to give birth to a new reality, a new life for everybody. And I would like to use her words again to show how painful the realization that his child that had been born under such hardships had a serious defects.

> Über lange Zeit weigerte ich mich zu glauben, die Fehler der Revolution seien nicht zu korrigieren, dazu war ich ihr zu sehr verbunden. Meine Liebe war nicht blind, doch nachsichtig und bedingungslos, wie die Liebe einer Mutter, die die Ausrutscher ihrer Tochter sieht, doch voller Vertrauen ist, dass ihr mütterlicher Geist schließlich siegen wird. (Belli 2002: 392. Translation: For a long time I refused to believe that the defects of the revolution were not corrigible. My love was not blind, but lenient and unconditional, like the love of a mother, who can see the mistake of her daughter but is full of confidence that her motherly spirit will win in the end.)

So paradoxically, the loss of power only for the first time created the possibilities for these activists to speak up freely, without being held back and/or holding themselves back for the purpose of the joint struggle and misunderstood loyalty. Margaret Randall, who was living in Nicaragua from 1980 to 1984, expressed her moment of "enlightenment" that took place at a Sandinista solidarity conference in 1991, with the members of the national directorate chairing it. Randall illustrates how she realized that they were all men; but more decisively, for the first time made "reference to the lack of feminist understanding, the fear of feminist ideas that characterizes most of these men" (Randall 1994: xi). Finally, she felt empowered in a new atmosphere of equality, of flat hierarchies, of a power structure closer to the revolutionary ideal society than it has ever been in place during the period of Sandinista leadership. "Like my Nicaraguan sisters, I now felt able to publicly express concerned criticism of these leaders. Now that they had become ordinary individuals, rather than the revered representatives of a revolution in power, it was easier to say these things" (Randall 1994: xi). Randall's wording gives an important insight to what had happened after the lost elections: those (mostly) men who have been seen as heroes for all these years, by their heroic status elevated beyond the rest of the population, could finally be seen as "normal" people - a development that definitely contributed to the partial flattening of the party's structure. At least, it opened a space for criticism from the inside - a criticism that is not possible to be voiced against "official" heroes.

II.3.4 A different vision

> (W)e women are conscious that we're not struggling for ourselves alone; we're struggling for men as well, and for our children, for all of humanity. And we've got a holistic vision of change. (Zamora in Randall 1994: 122)

In her interview with Margaret Randall, Michele Najlis tells an inspiring story of her friend and colleague Vidaluz Meneses, who had been offered to become Dean of Humanities at the prestigious Jesuit University in the Nicaraguan capital Managua (UCA). Instead of jumping at this unique chance, Najlis quotes Meneses telling the president "I'll have to think it over. I'll let you know in a week" (Najlis in Randall 1994: 64). She wanted to see if there are other qualified women around who would also deserve the job. After a while she came back with her answer that included an offer the president could not deflect:

> I'm willing to take the position. But I've found two other women who are equally qualified. We've talked among ourselves, and we're all comfortable with any of us being given the job. [...] We've also decided that whomever you decide to name, the other must immediately be made advisers to that position. (Najlis in Randall 1994: 64)

This amazing story shows how a totally different concept of power is emerging out of a new feminist consciousness in Nicaragua. Najlis goes as far as to say that "(h)ere at UCA, we have our own little matriarchy" (Najlis in Randall 1994: 64). Needless to say that matriarchy in this sense does not mean women exercising power over men, but is an expression for this new understanding of power that, according to Najlis, is a direct outcome of the empowerment of women in Nicaragua. Meneses herself explains the power concept she was basing her decision on as coming from her deeply rooted Christianity: "el poder como servicio, el poder desligado del autoritarismo, el poder como motivacion y no como mandato" (Menedes 2000; translation: power as service, power detached from authoritarianism, power as motivation and not as a mandate). Meneses speaks about a power concept based on what Joachim Bauer called the real motivation of human actions: the human desire to be loved and respected. By demanding the two other qualified women in her university as her advisers, Meneses opted for cooperation rather than competition, creating a win-win-situation in the sense that instead of maybe having created two "enemies" out of being disregarded, she found two supporters and colleagues who help her deal with the difficult tasks of her new position. The hierarchical structure of a traditional, catholic university has been flattened with a very simple "trick": to only accept the appointment as dean if two other women would be elevated to (almost) the same hierarchical level. The new cooperative leadership style produces results and creates a network of support which favors creativity as Najlis knows: "Vidaluz is dean of humanities, all four faculties have women chairs, and I'm Head of Culture. And we help each other out; we're always inventing things together. If one of us has important information, we share it with the others" (Najlis in Randall 1994: 64). Najlis makes clear that this new leadership style is contrary to what its protagonists have learned in their childhood and youth. "We were taught to be jealous of each other, to try to get ahead at other's expense" (Najlis in Randall 1994: 64).

The story about the "little matriarchy" at the UCA is a beautiful proof of the idea that evolution does not necessarily happen through the *struggle for life* or, in other words, competition. It also proves Riane Eisler right who states that the transformation from domination to partnership is possible. In the end, it's a matter of personal choice - but to come to that choice, to be able to choose cooperation instead of competition, is likely a direct consequence of a revolution that aspired to build a more humane and equal society.

It cannot be mentioned often enough that this new feminist vision of power and living together came directly from the revolutionary ideals. The idea that persons totally different in their visions and ideals can communicate and cooperate, that this is the only way how a society based on equality and real democracy can be achieved, developed out of the Dionysian experience of the successful liberation struggle - successful because of this relational way of dealing with each other's differences, so that collective energy could be accumulated that made the historical success possible. This notion was taken up by feminists and led to a different kind of vision for the future, as Vargas tells us:

> It wasn't until after the elections that we began getting together on our own, without the men, that we really began talking about the issues. And we generated a profound discussion - sometimes a bit violent, at other times on a higher plane - with women who continued not to understand where we're coming from: it was a discussion in which important ideas were expressed. And we began to understand what we needed to do in order to find a way to remain united while still recognizing these different ideas. That's when we came up with the phrase *Unidas en la Diversidad* (United in Difference). (Vargas in Randall 1994: 140)

This last quote has a lot in common with the Nietzschean expression of the Dionysian ideal of harmony within a crowd of different voices.

II.4 Idealization

Before coming to the concluding remarks of this book, I would like to make one last point, which has to do with the reception of the revolution outside of Nicaragua. Following the structure of this book, I will show one individual experience of a "Western" visitor of Nicaragua after the revolution on the example of Dietmar Schönherr, an Austrian-born actor and writer, stressing once again that the big international political structures are not the topic of this book. If they were, there would be a lot to say of the demonization of a little country in the backyard of the USA in a time still characterized by the mythological battle of two so-called superpowers both striving to rule the world. In other words, we are talking about the Cold War when proxy wars in the then so-called third world were just one rule of the game. I discussed this topic relating to Nicaragua as a grand example of covered influence and instrumentalisation of people in regards to the US-financed CIA-supported contra-war in my term paper for the Peace, Conflict and Development Master Program in Castellón, Spain (2006).

I also want to state that it is at least interesting that the best-known benevolent eye-witness accounts of Nicaragua in the years of Sandinista administration (at least those well-known in the German-speaking world) are written by men and therefore give us a good example of the male gaze on a revolution that considered itself to be a "revolution of love", an additive that was taken very serious by and, coming to the point of this chapter, romanticized by the Nicaragua solidarity movements in Western Europe and especially in Germany, Austria, and Switzerland.

Dietmar Schönherr traveled to Nicaragua for the first time in his life in 1985, after he had met Ernesto Cardenal, the priest-poet and Cultural Minister, in Germany and was invited by him. He published a book called *Nicaragua, mi amor* (1986) as a kind of travel diary. The book is about a man getting to know a totally different world, it seems, and he watches this different world with the eyes of a complete stranger since he doesn't even understand the language yet.

His testimonial is full of idealizations and romantic ideas and he is first of all amazed about the accessibility of the (male) party leaders and their unique readiness to talk to him and even show him around the country. Their cultural knowledge and artistic skills (almost all of them are writing poetry themselves) impresses him deeply. He starts to love the country and its people almost unconditionally, and he feels that the "new man" is emerging here, in the middle of nowhere. It seems that he came with a fixed image to Nicaragua, a myth à la David and Goliath, where a little country stood up against the imperialist superpower trying to defeat it.

The "revolution of love" he wanted to find he is finding everywhere. Different from other sources, he doesn't see the growing disappointment and discontent of people with their revolution (as has been shown, different sources - Randall, 1994; Bayard de Volo, 2001; Lancaster, 1992 - as well as Nicaraguan intellectuals themselves talk about the observation that the public opinion started to disapprove the FSLN's policies from 1985 onwards). But Schönherr feels it totally different; for him, this country is still full of brave and heroic people who try to build a better world. He describes his feelings when he visits the areal of the cultural ministry, which is situated in the former residence of the Somoza family:

> Kulturpolitik der Stille, der Milde, der Liebe, wie es Ernesto sagt: Die Revolution ist die Liebe. Das Grauen ist weggefegt, einfach rausgekehrt worden. Hier wächst etwas ganz Zartes, Verletzbares, etwas Wunderbares, das man nicht beschreiben kann, aber du spürst es ganz stark." (Schönherr 1986: 23. Translation: Cultural policy of tranquility, of mildness, of love, how Ernesto is saying: The revolution is love. The horror has vanished, has just been swept off. Here, something tender, vulnerable, something wonderful is growing that cannot be described, but you can feel it so intensely.)

Schönherr is overwhelmed by the combination of culture, art, love, and heroism he finds. As an artist himself, he feels extremely attracted to this new kind of politicians. Not being able to speak with the people first hand, he seems to keep on seeing what he was hoping to find. Even his aversion against heroic patriotism (an attitude very common in Germany and Austria, where patriotism has become something to be ashamed of since World War II) is melting away when a group of Nicaraguans is singing the national anthem, which the hymn of the FSLN has become: "Ich fange an, Heroisches zu ertragen. Da singen Brüder und Schwestern miteinander ein Lied, und wenn sie vom Tod singen, lachen ihre Augen immer noch." (Schönherr 1986: 30. Translation: I start to stand heroism. Here, brothers and sisters are singing a song together, and even when they are singing about death, their eyes are still laughing.) Schönherr's subjective notice stands in sharp contrast to the intensifying war and the emerging anti-war movements Bayard de Volo for example described. From a distance of more than 20 years, this innocent statement seems indeed like a rather pretentious judgment. He is talking about a people involved in a civil war fueled from the outside that is splitting families, friends apart; about a people suffering under economic embargos and the continuous killing of its sons. And the only thing he realizes about that is the smile people have when singing about death.

And indeed, his motives for such admiration and also for deciding soon after that he will actively take part in this endeavor to create a utopian new world inhabited by new men (and women?) sharing equally what they have and living independently from the powerful imperialist states have a lot to do with the void he feels right after traveling back to Germany.

> Ich wandere durch die Glitzerwelt aufgeplusterten und überflüssigen Wohlstands [...] In der Nacht fällt kein Regen Dach, am Tag plagt dich die Hitze nicht, [...] die Kinder haben keine aufgeblähten Bäuche. Und auf einmal wird dir klar, dass dort das Leben ist, wo die Widerstände sind, die Not, der Kampf ums nackte Überleben - und hier bist du tot wie eine tote Flunder. (Schönherr 1986: 24. Translation: I am wandering through the glamour world full of fluffed up and unnecessary prosperity [...]. In the night no rain is falling through the roof, during the day the heat doesn't afflict you, [...] the children don't have swollen bellies. And all out of a sudden you realize, that the life is there, where the

resistances are, the misery, the struggle for bare survival - and here you are dead like a dead fluke.)

To Schönherr's credit it has to be said that after writing down his memories, he returned to Nicaragua with money collected in Germany, and he stayed for months to help with his own hands building up the entire community structures of a village brought into life through the resettlement policies of the government - 400 people, half of which were children, were resettled after several contra-attacks had destroyed the old village's sustenance and killed a significant number of its inhabitants. With his support, the village got huts, a school, a church, and a small factory for agricultural equipment. His vision to create this ideal community and then give a number of orphans from other parts of the country a home within it couldn't be realized after all, but the *Project Posolera* seemed to be a success in the beginning.

His personal account though can be seen as nothing else than a proof of what Ervin Laszlo and other system theorists are claiming, namely that the immense emptiness in European / Western cultures since the Dionysian element, the energetic principle was stigmatized as something evil and pushed out led to this uncritical adoption of Nicaragua after the revolution as the ideal society. As Laszlo points out (Chapter I.4.2), the scientific world view with its drive for ever more specialized knowledge cannot fulfill our desire for wholeness and connectedness - with nature, with our fellow human beings, and last but not least, with ourselves. In German, we say that we don't feel ourselves any more when we do something stupid or even when we feel depressed and are lacking a meaning, a motivation in our life. This fatal apathy that Laszlo et al. detect in our comfort zone where everything is under control, we go to the supermarket when we are hungry and turn on the heating when we are cold, doesn't give us any reason to fight, for whatever higher goal. I would opt to interpret Schönherr's emotional statement that life is where misery, hunger, lack is, in this sense. It is obvious that sleeping in a barrack with rain coming through the roof in the night will make it easier to feel yourself - to feel connected with nature; with the people you share this life with, and with your own body under difficult physical circumstances. To feel alive in this sense, Schönherr is putting up with sharing the life of these people, valuing the goals of the revolution better than his own survival it seems, while he cannot know if and when the next contra-attack will take place. He writes about answering the question of his wife "is it dangerous?" on the telephone with "of course it's dangerous!" and it feels like he is enjoying his own heroism a bit too much.

The sequence of Nietzsche comes to mind again, when he describes Dionysianism: Individuals come and go, but the chorus will always be there. It seems that this feeling to be part of something greater than oneself, the common struggle against a vicious enemy, and the warmth of the community that integrated him as one of them was fulfilling the desire for this crucial part of human nature that is not honored any more in our western culture.

Thus overwhelmed by this new experience of a self-sufficient community, Schönherr seems to disregard the other, the Apollonian part of human nature, which wants to thrive individually. The German Marxist magazine MSZ calls him elitist when he doesn't appreciate the community's wish for one community TV set (MSZ 1988). Although the magazine's criticism reads quite cynical, I would argue that it has a point thinking about Schönherr's way to praise the artistic nature of the Nicaraguan people, who seem to be so much more interested in their own poetry and songs than in something as a TV that would fry their brains: "Es ist unbeschreiblich schön, wie diese Menschen mit ihren Dichtern leben, wie sie zuhören und lachen, wie da Liebe zum Ausdruck kommt" (Schönherr 1986: 31. Translation: It is indescribably beautiful, how these people live with their poets, how they listen to them and laugh, how in that love is expressed).

The story of Schönherr's commitment in Nicaragua continues, as well as his love for this country which he calls his "second home". What did change, though, is his enthusiastic and almost naive appraisal of the revolutionary ideals. As if he felt the Dionysian ecstasy six years after the revolution took place, the transpersonal energy that empowers individuals to join forces and construct something new, he also went through a sobering experience afterwards. As he gave himself totally for the construction of this symbolic community, Posolera, he felt total disappointment and sheer despair when he had to realize that after the end of the revolutionary period, the community broke apart. Very similar to the Nicaraguan women I quoted in this book who talked about their world falling apart confronted with the electoral loss of the FSLN in 1990, he writes: "Ein Stück meines Lebens ist mir abhanden gekommen" (Schönherr 2000: 102. Translation: A part of my life got lost) when he travels back to Posolera only to find that his utopia doesn't exist anymore. Before he finds out that almost every family had sold their little piece of land and left for the city hoping to find a better life after the new government privatized almost everything, he remembers that one of his collaborators warned him that this was about to happen:

> Die Leute werden alles verkaufen, wenn die Gesetze es zulassen. Sie werden ihre paar Sachen packen und verschwinden, irgendwohin, wo sie glauben, ein leichtes, besseres Leben zu finden, wahrscheinlich in die Hauptstadt. Dort werden sie in Pappschachteln und Dosenblech-Hütten in übel riechenden Slums dahinvegetieren. Sie lieben dein Dorf nicht. Der einzige, der es liebt, bist du. (Schönherr 2000: 103. Translation: The people will sell everything, as soon as the laws will allow it. They will pack their few belongings and leave, go somewhere, where they believe to find an easy, better life, most likely in the capital. There, they will vegetate in cardboard- and tin-barracks in smelly slums. They don't love your village. The only one who loves it is you.)

This sobering experience led Schönherr to the conclusion that it's not enough to give people houses, but they also have to gain a sense of home (Schuster 1999). And something else had changed, too: the almost exclusive focus on male protagonists, as it is so obvious in *Nicaragua, mi amor* (1985) shifted a bit towards women's lives in his second book on Nicaragua *Die blutroten Tomaten der Rosalia Morales* (2000). Not only is a woman now present in the title of the book (a female subject rather than the lovable object Nicaragua seems to represent in the first book), she is also playing a significant role in the story.

Another interesting example of the romanticized revolution is a Nicaraguan autobiographic novel written by one of the revolution's leaders, Omar Cabezas. The book that tells the story of Cabezas as guerrillero before the victory, originally titled *La montana es algo más que una inmensa estepa verde* (1982. Translation: The mountains are something more than a huge green steppe), got published in English, rather sticking to its original title as *Fire from the Mountain: The Making of a Sandinista.* But in German, the same book was published with a totally different title: *Die Erde dreht sich zärtlich, Companera* (1983. Translation: The earth is revolving tenderly, Companera). This title, clearly aimed at the "revolution of love", is, according to Andreas Goosses' enlightening essay *Die Erde dreht sich männlich, Companero* (Goosses 2000. Translation: The earth is revolving masculinely, Companero) misleading the German-speaking readers. The book was celebrated by the international solidarity movement. Sure enough, Goosses reveals it as an important contribution for the heroic self-conception of the male revolutionary, reproducing a number of Latin American masculinity stereotypes. "Sein Fazit ist niederschmetternd: Es wird hier ein traditionelles, militaristisches und machistisches Bild des Neuen Menschen bzw. Neuen Mannes (denn Frauen kommen sehr wenig vor) tradiert - und wurde offensichtlich sowohl in Lateinamerika als auch in Deutschland kaum hinterfragt" (Held 2000. Translation: His conclusion is staggering: Here, a traditional, militaristic and machistic picture of the New Man respectively the New Male (since women are almost non-existent in the book) is passed on - which obviously has barely been questioned in Latin America as in Germany).

Cabezas' account doesn't mention a lot of women. While reading it, I was wondering if the stories that at least 30% of the guerrilla fighters were women are true at all... there is not a single word about women in the mountains. Cabezas rarely mentions his "woman", the woman he had a relationship with before he left for the mountains, and he mentions his sexual appetite and that he doesn't know how to deal with it first with no woman around. But once, when he writes about being sent back to the city for medical treatment, there is a paragraph that can be seen as a perfect representation of the patriarchal world-view he was living in:

> [...], ich würde Claudia sehen. Und dann würde ich natürlich auch mit ihr schlafen und mich begeisterte der Gedanke, mit Claudia zu schlafen oder mit irgendeiner anderen Frau, das Gefühl, wieder eine Frau zu küssen, eine Frau zu streicheln, einer Frau mit der Hand über den ganzen Körper zu streichen, auf einer Frau zu liegen, der Orgasmus mit einer Frau, und ich dachte an die Frauen, die damals im Untergrund waren und ging sie in Gedanken der Reihe nach durch, welche gefiel mir vom Aussehen her am besten, nach Claudia, oder wenn Claudia mich nicht mehr liebte, welche Frau dann? (Cabezas 1982: 139f. Translation: [...], I would meet Claudia. And then, of course, I would also sleep with her and I was excited from the thought to sleep with Claudia or with whichever other woman, the feeling, to kiss a woman again, to fondle a woman, to run my hand over the whole body, to lie on top of a woman, the orgasm with a woman, and I thought of the women who were underground at that time and went through them one after the other in my thought, which one did I like best from her

looks, after Claudia, and if Claudia didn't love me anymore, which woman then?)

This quote is the first proof that there were, indeed, women in the guerilla, but in his daily accounts on fight training, marching, fighting, they didn't seem worth mentioning for Cabezas. What they are worth mentioning for is, as we can see, if they are considered as sex partners.

It is true, this paternalist attitude doesn't fit the book's German title and the solidarity movement didn't seem to question that either. Once again, the FSLN had to lose the elections, it seems, to make a critical stance from the outside possible. But then, again, it's never so easy to judge, and it shouldn't be. It is important to keep Riane Eisler's words in mind that the partnership society she is envisioning is not a utopian society nobody every makes mistakes or where violence doesn't exist. In this sense, Cabezas' book can also be understood as an honest life story of a man who grew up in a certain society, was socialized in a certain way, and who tried his very best to go beyond his origin, to go beyond himself.

THE DREAM ALIVE

"We can't give up dreaming, even if it sounds romantic and obsolete. And when you live in a country like Nicaragua, you know it's particularly important to hold onto the dream" (Belli in Randall: 186). Gioconda Belli's tenacious holding onto the dream of a different, better Nicaragua and consequently, a better world is a strong symbol for the new consciousness and strength women gained in the framework of the Nicaraguan revolution. Her poems and especially her novel - *Waslala* (1999), which tells a fantastic story of a country full of misery, exploited by imperialist forces that not only take the country's riches but even dump their garbage in it and about a dream that became an inherent part of the country's storytelling and myth world, a tale about a utopian community where dreams are reality - seem to cry out at the people to keep the hope alive, to not forget that there once was a time when dreams were lived up to and everything seemed possible. She is proud to be born in a country of poets and dreamers, of visionaries, and she seems convinced that once upon a time, the transformation of the social order will be completed.

Reading the news about Nicaragua these days is frustrating. Since Daniel Ortega is once again the president of Nicaragua (he formally took office in January, 2007), it became clear all and for once that the FSLN developed into a political party similar to most political parties that are striving to be in power. Their understanding of power is of the old kind, and not of the new, partnership-oriented power as responsibility. As Elaine Meyers stated in her analysis of the 100th monkey story, it's important to understand that the old generations will not be the ones to readily take up a new vision. Daniel Ortega, who was accused by his stepdaughter of having abused her sexually, will most likely not be the outstanding personality who can lead his people into a bright and just future.

But it's not only Ortega's personality that makes reading the news about Nicaragua frustrating. It is the overwhelming power of the international system that seems once again to squeeze everything out of that little country, which is there. Since Nicaragua was one of the "winners" of debt relief in 2005, it had to sign contracts, which request it to compromise even more of its social system. The glorious times of the literacy crusade come to mind. Where are these heroes today, the young, enthusiastic masses?

But yet, not everything is negative. Things have changed since 1990, and today, there is a strong and committed women's movement in the country, and there are people, especially women, who dare to speak up against any autocratic attempt. And there is, still, a majority of people in this country who know that they have rights, and that they fought for those rights with their blood and sweat. These people know that education is a right, and that human rights exist. I got to know the Nicaraguan people as a highly politicized reflected people, and as a people prepared to take their destiny in their own hands. Yes, they may have lost their belief in politicians. But there is something in this country, a feeling, indefinable, that the hope is still there, and the fighting spirit is still there, and the overwhelming wisdom of the power of individuals.

Still, the weak point I tried to show in the present publication, which lies in the interpersonal relations, the families, the gender relations, is not resolved. And how could it be with structures in place that once again enhanced dependency relationships, unequal gender relations, and even led to the growing up of another generation where boys were sent to school and girls had to stay home. But the seed of change is still there, in the hearts and minds of people, since the knowledge of a different possibility, a common dream, has been implanted in the collective unconscious of these people and is living forth in the conscious part through the stories of those who experienced it and the arts that are so honored in this country: poems, novels, and music.

Gioconda Belli's poem *The Dream Bearers* is a striking document about the dreams that, once shared by a critical mass of people in a system, can never be silenced again.

The Dream Bearers

In all the prophecies the destruction of the world is written.

All the prophecies foretell humanity creating its own destruction.

But time and life endlessly renewed also engendered a generation of lovers and dreamers; men and women who dreamed not of the world's destruction, but of building a world of butterflies and nightingales.

From an early age, they were branded by love. Behind their everyday appearance they hid tenderness and the midnight sun. Their mothers often found them crying over a dead bird and years later, found many of them dead, too, like birds.

These beings lived with translucid women and left them impregnated with honey and children who grew like grass under the caress of rainy days.

This is how the dream bearers multiplied in the world, fiercely attacked by those who bore catastrophic prophecies. They were called deluded romantics, inventors of utopias. They were told their words were old - which was true, since paradise has been an ancient memory in the heart of humanity. Those who accumulated riches feared them, and hurled their armies against them.

But every night the dream bearers made love, and their seed continued growing in the wombs of women who not only bore dreams but multiplied them, and made them run and speak.

This is how the world engendered its life again
just as it had engendered those who invented the way to extinguish the sun.

The dream bearers survived the cold climates, but in the warm climates they seemed to sprout by spontaneous generation. Perhaps the palm trees, the blue skies, the torrential rains had something to do with this. The truth is that this specimens, like hardworking little ants, never stopped dreaming and building their beautiful worlds, worlds of brothers and sisters, of men and women who called each other companeros, who taught each other to read, consoled each other in times of death, healed and cared for each other, loved and helped each other in the art of loving and in the defense of happiness.

They were happy in their world of sugar and wind and people came from all directions to be impregnated by their breath and by their clear gazes and the people who had known them went out in all directions bearing dreams dreaming new prophecies that spoke of times of butterflies and nightingales in which the world would not have to end up in a hecatomb. On the contrary, scientists would design fountains, gardens, surprising toys to further humanity's happiness.

They are dangerous *read the message that rolled off the presses* They are dangerous *said the presidents in their speeches* They are dangerous *murmured the makers of war*

They must be destroyed *read the message that rolled off the presses* They must be destroyed *said the presidents in their speeches* They must be destroyed *murmured the makers of war.*

The dream bearers knew their power and therefore were not surprised.

And they also knew that life had engendered them to protect itself from the death announced in the prophecies. And so they defended their lives even with death.

And so they cultivated gardens of dreams and exported them tied with big colorful ribbons and the prophets of darkness spent days and nights watching the secret roots and roads searching for these dangerous shipments which they never succeeded in intercepting because the person with no eyes for dreaming cannot see dreams either by day or night.

And in the world a dream traffic has been unleashed that
the traffickers in death cannot stop; and everywhere
there are packages with big bows
that only this new race of people can see, and the seed of these
dreams cannot be detected because it is enclosed in red hearts or in
ample maternity dresses where tiny feet of dreamers teem inside the
wombs that bear them.

It is said that earth, after giving birth to them,
unchained a rainbow in the sky and blew the breath of
fertility on the roots of trees.

All we know is that we have seen them we know
that life engendered them as protection against
the prophecies of death.

(Belli 1989: 85-91)

BIBLIOGRAPHY

ABRAHAM, RALPH (1997): «Chaos and Erodynamics with Ralph Abraham.» In (eds. David Jay Brown & Rebecca McCLen Novick): *Mavericks of the Mind. Conversations for the New Millennium.* Internet Edition. Accessed on July 25th, 2007 at: http://www.levity.com/mavericks/

BARDINI, ROBERTO (2003): *Edén Pastora, un cero en la historia.* Movimiento Bambú. Accessed on September 8th at http://www.rodelu.net/bardini/bardini55.htm

BAUER, JOACHIM (2006): *Prinzip Menschlichkeit. Warum wir von Natur aus kooperieren.* Hoffmann und Kampe.

BAYARD DE VOLO, LORRAINE (2001): *Mothers of Heroes and Martyrs. Gender Identity Politics in Nicaragua, 1979-1999.* The John Hopkins University Press, Baltimore & London.

BELLI, GIOCONDA (2002): *Die Verteidigung des Glücks.* dtv, München.

BELLI, GIOCONDA (1994): «We were the knights of the round table.» In: (ed. Margaret Randall) *Sandino's Daughters Revisited: Feminism in Nicaragua.* Rutgers University Press, New Brunswick, New Jersey. 168-191.

BELLI, GIOCONDA (1989): *From Eve's Rib.* Curbstone Press, Willimantic.

BOULDING, ELISE (2000): *Cultures of Peace. The Hidden Side of History.* Syracuse University Press.

BOULDING, KENNETH and BOULDING, ELISE (1995): *The Future. Images and Processes.* Sage Publications, Beverly Hills.

BOULDING, KENNETH (1985^: *The World as a Total System.* Sage Publications Beverly Hills.

BURGESS, HEIDI; BURGESS, GUY (1997): «Transformative Approaches to Conflict.» *Conflict Research Consortium,* University of Colorado.
Accessed on December 3rd, 2006 at
http://www.colorado.edu/conflict/transform/index.html

CABEZAS, OMAR (1983): Die *Erde dreht sich zärtlich, Companera. Autobiographischer Bericht aus Nicaragua.* Peter Hammer Verlag, Wuppertal.

CHAPMAN, AH and M. CHAPMAN-SANTANA (1995): «The influence of Nietzsche on Freud's ideas», *The British Journal of Psychiatry,* vol. 166, no. 2,251-253.

CHINCHILLA, MIGUEL ANGEL (2007): «Vidaluz y la Brigada 'Leonel Rugama'» *El Nuevo Diario.* March 24, 2007. Accessed on August 7th, 2007 at:
http://www.elnuevodiario.com.ni/2007/03/24/suplemento/nuevoamanecer/5275

DARWIN, CHARLES (1871): *The Descent of Man.* Accessed on on July 10th, 2007 at:
http://www.infidels.org/library/historical/charles_darwin/descent_of_man/

DER SPIEGEL (20/08/1979): *Nicaragua: Barmherzig im Sieg.* 93, 96.

DIETRICH, WOLFGANG (1988): *Nicaragua. Entstehung, Charakter und Hoffnung eines neuen Weges.* Heidelberger Verlagsanstalt.

DIETRICH, WOLFGANG (2006a): «Peaces. An Aestetic Concept, a Moral Need or a Transrational Virtue?» *Asteriskos. Journal of International and Peace Studies.* 1/2: 25-45.

DIETRICH, WOLFGANG (2006b): «Apollinische Neurose.» *Planet.* Nr. 44/April 2006. Accessed on May 24th, 2007 at:
http://www.archiv.gruene.at/planet/planet44/index.php?seite=themen&tid=41627&PHPSESSID=c2befa28157a3cf4f6afe7f281310aae

EISLER, RIANE (1988): *The Chalice and the Blade. Our History, Our Future.* Harper San Francisco.

EISLER, RIANE (2004): «Pragmatopia: Revisioning Human Possibilities.)) *TIKKUN.* VOL. 19, NO. 6 - Nov/Dec 2004. Accessed on July 23rd, 2007 at: http://www.partnershipway.org/html/subpages/articles/pragmatopia.htm

GABBERT, K.; GABBERT, W. et.al. (eds.) (2000): «Editorial.» *Jahrbuch Lateinamerika. Geschlecht und Macht.* Westfälisches Dampfboot. Accessed on September 6th, 2007 at: http://www.jahrbuch-lateinamerika.de/jb-24.html

GARCIA MARQUEZ GABRIEL (2000): *Frei sein und unabhängig.* Kiepenheuer & Witsch, Köln.

GALTUNG, JOHAN (2000): *Conflict Transformation by Peaceful Means (the Transcend Method). Participants' Manual - Trainers' Manual.* United Nations Disaster Management Training Program.

HELD, LAURA (2000): «Männlichkeitswahn und Berufsfeministinnen. Geschlecht und Macht - Lateinamerika-Jahrbuch 2000.» *Ila-Web.* Accessed on September 6th, 2007 at http://www.ila-web.de/buchbesprechungen/buecher244.htm#M%C3%A4nnlichkeitswahn%20und%20Berufsfeministinnen

HELD, WERNER (2001): «Jung, Sheldrake und die Quantenphysik.» *Der Datadiwan. Die Datenbank für außergewöhnliches Wissen in der Ganzheitsmedizin und den Grenzgebieten der Wissenschaft.* Accessed on July 17th, 2007 at: http://www.datadiwan.de/netzwerk/index.htm?/experten/he_003d_.htm>.

JUNG, CARL GUSTAV (1964): «Zwei Schriften über Analytische Psychologie.» *7. Band des Gesamtwerks.* Olten.

JUNG, CARL GUSTAV (1975): «Die Bedeutung des Vaters für das Schicksal des Einzelnen.» In: *Der Einzelne in der Gesellschaft.* Walter Verlag, Olten und Freiburg im Breisgau.

JUNG, CARL GUSTAV (2004): «The Concept of the Collective Unconscious.» *The CG Jung Page.* Posted: 19.1.2004. Accessed on May 24th, 2007 at: http://www.cgjungpage.org/index.php?option=com_content&task=view&id=527&Itemid=40

KANT, IMMANUEL (1784): «An Answer to the Question: " What Is Enlightenment?"» In: *Modern History Sourcebook.* Accessed on July 16th, 2007 at http://www.fordham.edu/halsall/mod/kant-whatis.html

KAUFFMANN, VERONIKA (1997): *Toward A Dynamic Partnering Cosmology. A World in I-Thou - Partnership.* Accessed on July 19th, 2007 at http://www.gwu.edu/~asc/papers/tdpc.html

KENT, W.H. (1908): «Devil» In: *The Catholic Encyclopedia, Volume IV.* New York: Robert Appleton Company. Transcribed by Rick McCarthy. Accessed on August 13th, 2007 at http://www.newadvent.org/cathen/04764a.htm

KEYES, KEN JR. (1981): *The Hundredth Monkey.* Vision Books, Coos Bay, Oregon.

KREIS, STEVEN (2000): «Lecture 3: Nietzsche, Freud and the Thrust Toward Modernism (2).» *The History Guide. Lectures on Twentieth Century Europe.* Accessed on May 28th, 2007 at http://www.historyguide.org/europe/lecture3.html

LANCASTER, ROGER N. (1992): *Life is Hard. Machismo, Danger and the Intimacy of Power in Nicaragua.* University of California Press, Berkeley, Los Angeles, Oxford.

LASZLO, ERVIN (1972): *Introduction to Systems Philosophy. Toward a New Paradigm of Contemporary Thought.* Gordon and Breach, New York - London - Paris.

LAJOIE, D. H. and SHAPIRO, S. I. (1992): «Definitions of transpersonal psychology: The first twenty-three years.» *Journal of Transpersonal Psychology.* Vol. 24.

LEDERACH, JEAN PAUL (2005): *The Moral Imagination. The Art and Soul of Building Peace.* Oxford University Press, New York.

LEDERACH, JEAN PAUL (2003): *The Little Book of Conflict Transformation.* Good Books, Intercourse.

LEONHARD, RALF (2006): «Moralischer Bankrott einer Revolution.» *Südwind Magazin,* 12/2006, 14.

LOYE, DAVID (2004a): «Darwin, Maslow and the Fully Human Theory of Evolution.» In (ed. David Loye): *The Great Adventure. Toward a Fully Human Theory of Evolution.* Suny Series in Transpersonal and Humanistic Psychology, State University of New York Press.

LOYE, DAVID (2004b): *Darwin's Unfolding Revolution and the Liberation of the 21st Century.* Accessed on July 10th, 2007 at http://www.thedarwinproject.com/revolution/book/dur.pdf

LUCIAK, ILJA A. (1998): «Gender Equality and Electoral Politics on the Left: A Comparison of El Salvador and Nicaragua.» *Journal of Interamerican Studies and World Affairs.* Vol. 40, Nr. 1, 39-66.

LUZ, MENAHEM (1998): «Dionysus: Myth and Ritual in Sources of the Archaic Period.» In: (ed. R. Rosenthal-Heginbottom) *Dionysus and His Retinue in the Art of Ertetz-Israel,* Hecht Museum Catalogue 14 (1998), 52-56 (Eng,). Accessed on Mai 22nd, 2007 at http://research.haifa.ac.il/~mluz/dionysus.html

MENESES, VIDALUZ (2000): «Los intelectuales y el poder. Una perspectiva de genero.» In: *El Nuevo Diario,* February 4th, 2000. Accessed on August 1st on http://archivo.elnuevodiario.com.ni/2000/febrero/04-febrero-2000/opinion/opinion1.html

MENESES, VIDALUZ (1994): «As a woman, I think it was worth living the revolutionary process» In: (ed. Margaret Randall) *Sandino's Daughters Revisited: Feminism in Nicaragua.* Rutgers University Press, New Brunswick, New Jersey. 144-168.

MSZ MARXISTISCHE STREIT- UND ZEITSCHRIFT (1/1988): *Dietmar Schönherrs betroffene Solidarität: "NICARAGUA, MI AMOR"*. Verein zur Förderung des marxistischen Pressewesens e.V. München. Accessed on September 6th, 2007 on http://www.gegenstandpunkt.com/msz/html/88/88_1/nicarag.htm

MUNOZ, FRANCISCO (2005): *Imperfect Peace.* Accessed on July 20th, 2007 at http://www.ugr.es/~fmunoz/documentos/imperfectpeace.pdf

MYERS, ELAINE (1985): «The Hundreth Monkey Revisited.» *In Context. Strategies for Cultural Change* # 9, Spring 1985, p 10.

NAJLIS, MICHELE (1994): «Women's Solidarity has given our lives a new dimension: laughter.» In: (ed. Margaret Randall) *Sandino's Daughters Revisited: Feminism in Nicaragua.* Rutgers University Press, New Brunswick, New Jersey. Pp 40-67.

NIETZSCHE, FRIEDRICH (1999a): «The Birth of Tragedy» In: (eds. Raymond Geuss and Ronald Speirs) *The Birth of Tragedy And Other Writings.* Cambridge University Press.

NIETZSCHE, FRIEDRICH (1999b): «The Dionysiac World View» In: (eds. Raymond Geuss and Ronald Speirs) *The Birth of Tragedy And Other Writings.* Cambridge University Press.

POELLNER, PETER (2000): *Nietzsche and Metaphysics.* Oxford: Oxford University Press. Oxford Scholarship Online. Oxford University Press. Accessed on 28 May 2007 at <http://dx.doi.org/10.1093/0198250630.001.0001>

RANDALL, MARGARET (1994): *Sandino's Daughters Revisited: Feminism in Nicaragua.* Rutgers University Press, New Brunswick, New Jersey.

ROBERTSON, ROBIN (1995): *Jungian Archetypes. Jung, Gödel and the history of archetypes.* Nicolas-Hays, York Beach, Maine.

SCHNEIDER, ROBERT (2004): *Kristus. Das unerhörte Leben des Jan Beukels.* Aufbau Verlag.

SCHÖNHERR, DIETMAR (1986): *Nicaragua, mi amor. Tagebuch einer Reise und das Projekt Posolera.* Peter Hammer Verlag, Wuppertal.

SCHÖNHERR, DIETMAR (2000): *Die blutroten Tomaten der Rosalia Morales. Zweite erweiterte Liebeserklärung an eine unwirsche Geliebte.* Eichborn AG, Frankfurt am Main.

SCHUSTER, WERNER (1999): *Nicaragua mi amor.* Accessed on September 6th, 2007 on http://members.chello.at/werner-schuster/schoenherr.html

SCHÜTZHOFER, TIMM B. (2007): «Nicaragua: Ortegas Pakt mit dem Kardinal. Wie die Revolution ihre Seele verkaufte.» *Linkszeitung,* May 3rd 2007. Accessed on July 31st, 2007 at http://linkszeitung.de/content/view/109784/45/

SELBIN, ERIC (1999): *Modern Latin American Revolutions.* Westview Press, Boulder, Colorado.

SHELDRAKE, RUPERT (2005): «Morphic Fields and Morphic Resonance. An Introduction.» *Rupert Sheldrake Online.* Accessed on July 17th, 2007 at http://www.sheldrake.org/papers/Morphic/morphic_intro.html

SHELDRAKE, RUPERT; MCKENNA, TERENCE; ABRAHAM, RALPH (1993). *Denken am Rande des Undenkbaren. Über Ordnung und Chaos, Physik und Metaphysik, Ego und Weltseele.* Scherz Verlag, Bern, München, Wien.

SHELDRAKE, RUPERT (1995/6). «Hootenanny Editor Ken Weathersby talks with Rupert Sheldrake», *Hootenanny Magazine* # 3, Winter 1995/6. Accessed on July 17th, 2007 at http://www.hootenanny.com/hootenanny-archive/hootenanny-3-winter-19956/hootenanny-editor-ken-weathersby-talks-with-rupert-sheldrake/

SOKEL, WALTER HERBERT (2006): «On the Dionysian in Nietzsche. Monism and its Consequences», *Nietzsche Circle.* Accessed on 20/05/07 at http://www.nietzschecircle.com/Pdf/ON_DIONYSIAN_WH_SOKEL.pdf

SWEET, DENNIS (1999): «The Birth of The Birth of Tragedy», *Journal of the History of Ideas,*
vol. 60, no. 2, 345-359.

VARGAS, MILÚ (1994): «Our Experience in the FSLN is what gives us this strength.» In: (ed. Margaret Randall) *Sandino's Daughters Revisited: Feminism in Nicaragua.* Rutgers University Press, New Brunswick, New Jersey. 125-144.

WILES, DAVID (2000): *Greek Theatre Performance. An Introduction.* Cambridge University Press.

WILS, HOPP, ROPERS, VIMALARAJAH, ZUNZER (2006): «The Systemic Approach to Conflict Transformation. Concept and Fields of Application.» *Berghof Center for Peace Support.* Berlin.

ZAMORA, DAISY (1994): «I am Looking for the Women of my House.» In: (ed. Margaret Randall) *Sandino's Daughters Revisited: Feminism in Nicaragua.* Rutgers University Press, New Brunswick, New Jersey. 98125.

ZAMORA, DAISY (1993): *Clean Slate. New and selected poems.* Curbstone Press, Willimantic.

http://www.hospitalityclub.org/hc/travel_information.php?wgInfo=Nicaragua:@:Attractions_and_Things_to_See_and_Do; accessed on 1.4.2007

Die kommende Demokratie
hrsg. von Wolfgang Dietrich (Universität Innsbruck)

Daniel Hausknost
Weg ist das Ziel
Zur Dekonstruktion der Ökologiebewegung
Ist die Schaffung einer sauberen Umwelt nicht eigentlich der Kardinalfehler einer emanzipatorischen Bewegung, indem dadurch gerade die sichtbaren Symptome verschwinden, die uns daran erinnern, dass dieses System nicht funktioniert? Verfügt die Umweltbewegung denn noch über eine strategische Perspektive; hat sie jemals über eine solche verfügt? Und bedeutet erfolgreicher Umweltschutz nicht letztlich die Herstellung der perfekten Illusion, die Narkotisierung des Politischen? Dieses Buch geht der Frage nach, wie das politische Projekt der Ökologiebewegung neu formuliert werden könnte.
Bd. 1, 2005, 176 S., 19,90 €, br., ISBN 3-8258-8500-3

Dialog
Beiträge zur Friedensforschung

Österreichisches Studienzentrum für Frieden und Konfliktlösung (Hg.)
Die Weltunordnung von Ökonomie und Krieg
Von den gesellschaftlichen Verwerfungen der neoliberalen Globalisierung zu den weltumspannenden politischen Ansätzen jenseits des Casinokapitalismus. Projektleitung: Thomas Roithner
Bd. 49, 3. Aufl.. 2008, 304 S., 12,90 €, br., ISBN 978-3-8258-9723-9

Österreichisches Studienzentrum für Frieden und Konfliktlösung (Hg.)
Gute Medien – Böser Krieg?
Medien am schmalen Grat zwischen Cheerleadern des Militärs und Friedensjournalismus. Projektleitung: Thomas Roithner
Bd. 52, 2007, 176 S., 9,80 €, br., ISBN 978-3-8258-0137-3

Österreichisches Studienzentrum für Frieden und Konfliktlösung (Hg.)
Krisenherd Naher und Mittlerer Osten
Eine Region am Rande des Flächenbrands mit realistischer Friedensperspektive? Friedensbericht 2007. Projektleiter: Ronald H. Tuschl
Bd. 53, 2007, 264 S., 9,80 €, br., ISBN 978-3-8258-0138-0

Österreichisches Studienzentrum für Frieden und Konfliktlösung (Hg.)
Von kalten Energiestrategien zu heißen Rohstoffkriegen?
Schachspiel der Weltmächte zwischen Präventivkrieg und zukunftsfähiger Rohstoffpolitik im Zeitalter des globalen Treibhauses. Projektleitung: Thomas Roithner
Bd. 54, 2008, 312 S., 9,80 €, br., ISBN 978-3-8258-0931-7

Österreichisches Studienzentrum für Frieden und Konfliktlösung (Hg.)
Die Neue Weltordnung in der Krise
Von der uni- zur multipolaren Weltordnung? Friedensbericht 2008
Bd. 55, 2008, 264 S., 9,80 €, br., ISBN 978-3-8258-1450-2

Österreichisches Studienzentrum für Frieden und Konfliktlösung (Hg.)
Globale Armutsbekämpfung – ein Trojanisches Pferd?
Auswege aus der Armutsspirale oder westliche Kriegsstrategien? Projektleitung: Thomas Roithner
Bd. 56, 2. 2009, 368 S., 9,80 €, br., ISBN 978-3-8258-1762-6

Österreichisches Studienzentrum für Frieden und Konfliktlösung (Hg.)
Auf dem Weg zum neuen Kalten Krieg?
Vom neuen Antagonismus zwischen West und Ost. Friedensbericht 2009. Ergebnisse der State-of-Peace-Konferenz 2009. Projektleitung: Ronald H. Tuschl
Welche Weltpolitik verfolgen die USA nach den Präsidentschaftswahlen bezüglich Umwelt, Sicherheit und Energiepolitik? Strebt Russland eine Rolle in der Weltordnung an, die eine neue Polarität zwischen West und Ost provoziert bzw. inwieweit wird diese vom Westen mitverschuldet? Kann Europa dabei ausgleichend auf die beiden Hemisphären einwirken oder fällt dieses stattdessen in die Rolle des einstigen Kalten Krieges zurück? Welche Rolle spielt die NATO bei der globalen Militarisierung? Welche friedenspolitischen Implikationen ergeben sich aus der Verknappung der Ressourcen? Inwieweit entwickelt sich das weltumspannende Datennetz zum neuen digitalen Kampfraum zwischen Ost und West? Welchen Einfluss hat die jüngste internationale Finanzkrise auf die aktuellen friedenspolitischen Geschehnisse bzw. inwieweit entwickelt sich die transnationale Unternehmensregulation zum politisch umkämpften Terrain? Welche Möglichkeiten und Mittel stehen dabei den Vereinten Nationen zur Verfügung, um einen neuen Kalten Krieg zu verhindern? All diesen Fragen wurde auf der heurigen State-of-Peace-Konferenz 2009 auf den Grund gegangen, deren Ergebnisse in diesem Friedensbericht dokumentiert sind.
Bd. 57, 2009, 312 S., 9,80 €, br., ISBN 978-3-643-50061-8

LIT Verlag Berlin – Münster – Wien – Zürich – London
Auslieferung Deutschland / Österreich / Schweiz: siehe Impressumsseite